NCSS *in Retrospect*

O. L. Davis, Jr., *Editor*

BULLETIN 92

National Council for the Social Studies
Founded 1921

Editorial staff on this publication: *Michael Simpson, Terri S. Ackerman, Paul Degnan*
Editorial services provided by *Lynn Page Whittaker*, Charles River Press
Production Manager: *Gene Cowan*
Designer: *Paul Wolski*

Library of Congress Catalog Card Number: 95-071964
ISBN 0-87986-068-5

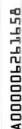

NCSS *In Retrospect*

contents

Toward Celebration and Continuance
An Invitation to Reflection

O. L. Davis, Jr.
The University of Texas at Austin

ANNIVERSARIES MARK REMEM-
BRANCES. OFTEN, THEY SPARKLE
with celebration. They are also occasions to
pause and take stock, even in the midst of antic-
ipation. Many anniversaries resemble family
reunions. They honor special people, relationships, and events that are only dimly known
except through the rich stories that make the
past breathe and laugh and cry in the present.

The year 1995 marks a very special anniversary in American education: it is the seventy-
fifth year of the life of the National Council
for the Social Studies (NCSS).

Seventy-five years. What a very long time!
Likely, no present NCSS member taught in
an American school seventy-five years ago when
the organization began its work. Not many of
us members personally remember hearing the
awesome news of the Hiroshima blast and
the subsequent peal of bells that signaled V-J
Day fifty Augusts ago. Many current members
were not alive when the first space satellite blast-
ed into space in 1957. NCSS continues to outlive
its membership.

NCSS does not simply survive, nor merely
exist. It continues for a simple reason: it serves.
It has served since it began.

NCSS has provided information about what
and how social studies teachers have taught and
might teach in their classrooms. Through *Social
Education*, its journal, and in other publications,
it regularly has offered new substantive insights
from history and geography, from government,
economics and other fields. Its publications
have offered information about fresh topics in
the several social studies, and have also provided
descriptions of, as well as admonitions about,
teaching practices. They have suggested means
by which students can become more actively

engaged with important ideas and concepts. They have highlighted new possibilities for emphasis in classrooms. Through its annual meetings, special conferences, and innovative programs, NCSS has made available to its members a great variety of opportunities to extend their knowledge, their sensitivities, and, yes, also their skills. NCSS has been important for social studies teachers in remote and urban schools, as well as for teachers in proudly conventional or traditional programs and in enterprisingly innovative programs. It has contributed both to teachers who stress multidisciplinary and social problem-centered studies and to teachers who seldom utter the term "social studies."

I can attest that NCSS serves because I know and have taught with many individuals whom it has served. NCSS also has served me well in very personal ways.

I joined NCSS when I was an eighth-grade teacher. I enjoyed reading *Social Education* each month, and was stunned that its editor welcomed a book review from me, a young and certainly unknown classroom teacher. Over the years, like some other members, I submitted manuscripts to the journal; most were rejected. I still welcome *Social Education* each month. I first attended an annual meeting in Kansas City more than thirty-five years ago. At that meeting, I met individuals from across the nation—some established mandarins in the field; others, like me, newcomers. Some friendships blossomed from that meeting and continue to this day.

In addition, I have been fortunate to know and work with a number of NCSS leaders from enthusiastic classroom teachers to officers. Of the several NCSS Presidents I have known, two were my graduate school teachers, both professors of history. NCSS members and leaders, I have found, enjoy fruitful exchanges of ideas. Annual meetings never fail to provide opportunities for me to meet and talk with other professionals who share my interests and

concerns. I have attended other annual meetings but never as regularly as I have wished. Still, over most of them, I remember special individuals who delivered major speeches, small group meetings that I attended, and ideas that sprang to mind as a result of my interactions. I especially remember President Harry Truman's speech at my first annual meeting. He began by asking us teachers the constitutional title of the presiding judge of the U.S. Supreme Court. Then, he stopped his address and asked us to talk with one another. That night, none of us at my table knew the answer. After President Truman's speech, none of us forgot it. NCSS continues to help me learn. I am confident that it benefits other members in similar as well as in very different ways.

Across the years, some NCSS members wished it to do more, and others lamented that it tried as much as it did. At times, the organization has been silent on matters of great moment and squandered opportunities to lead. On other occasions, it has staked out and vigorously supported prominent and right-minded positions. At some meetings, its delegates have debated what many considered trivial issues, but they almost always deliberate on truly significant motions as well. From time to time, NCSS programs have included attention to simplistic notions, but they always have featured sessions that treated profound concerns as well.

NCSS also serves the role of the social studies in American schools. It continues to share with other groups of Americans the trusteeship of the common good of citizenship in this republic.

Undoubtedly, NCSS will never do enough or grow large enough or be visible enough or be influential enough to satisfy all the interests of its diverse membership. It shares the common lot of the public schools and the American democracy which it serves. Simply, good is never good enough. Still, seventy-five years in pursuit of improved and increasingly robust social studies programs in American schools constitutes impressive achievement.

The occasion of this special anniversary, a diamond jubilee, prompted this bulletin. Such practices are commonplace within scholarly communities. Sometimes, the celebratory volume is a history of the group. This booklet clearly is not that history. Without question, NCSS needs a proper historical study of its work. It would fill an important gap in the knowledge of American education and, certainly, about NCSS itself. However, this volume is not an organizational history, even though it will be useful to any such undertaking.

Rather than limit NCSS history to celebration, this celebratory volume contributes to that history. Its central purpose is to inform. Toward this end, information and interpretation in the chapters are meant to extend and deepen what individuals already remember and think about NCSS. Too commonly, individuals' and the Council's sense of history poorly serves both NCSS and the social studies field. *NCSS in Retrospect* is designed not only to inform but to remind current members and other education professionals of some of the organization's contributions during a crucial seventy-five year period of American history. The volume does not intend to correct memory. Rather, it hopes to illuminate dimensions of NCSS activities and to foster renewal of commitment to the Council's long-held purposes.

This volume does something else. Through the considered experience of several NCSS members, this bulletin offers a set of thoughtful interpretations of major elements of NCSS's history. As such projects go, it likely misses some aspects that merit inclusion. The original plan surely overlooked some topics; some planned essays fell by the wayside. Nevertheless, the chapters provide substantial individual reflections on a number of important issues and activities.

Authors include several former Presidents. Other authors have served NCSS in different capacities. All have been members for most of their careers. However, they do not necessarily agree either in their understanding of the Council's past or in their visions of its future. For years, some have sharply contested the interpretations and proposals advanced by others. They are united, however, in their loyalty to NCSS. Their chapters profited from the richness of their intimate personal knowledge of NCSS and their long commitment to vigorous, mindful, social studies practice. Their essays glitter with their distinctive voices. Deliberately, they are personal, not consensual, statements. They point to moments of glory as well as to disfiguring warts. The variety of these retrospective essays honors the nature of individuality and honest expression that NCSS always has fostered. Certainly, the authors have left much unwritten; others will discover and write more in the future. Still, as they remind a new generation of members about NCSS's past, they seek to stimulate thought about its continuing, creative evolution.

NCSS in Retrospect offers a measure of observance and celebration of seventy-five years of the Council's presence and service to American education. Its contents will inform most NCSS members and may surprise some. Most of all, it invites NCSS members to spend some time in reflecting about their professional association. Knowing something of its rich past should enable current and future members together to invent its even richer future. The vitality of NCSS truly celebrates the gift of its past to its future.

NCSS The Early Years

Stephen J. Thornton
Teachers College, Columbia University

THE TITLE OF THIS CHAPTER IS DECEPTIVELY STRAIGHTFORWARD. Neither the date when the National Council for the Social Studies (NCSS) was established nor what constitutes its "early years" is self-evident. Rather, like the emergence of a component of the curriculum labeled "social studies," over a lengthy period of time, NCSS evolved into something recognizably similar to today's organization. Moreover, the evolution of NCSS, as we shall see, reveals a great deal about what Ellen Condliffe Lagemann (1989) terms the "politics of knowledge." At the opening of the twentieth century, no one could have confidently predicted that a professional association along the lines of NCSS would develop.

In this chapter, I present one perspective on how NCSS was established and how it found its feet as an organization. As O. L. Davis, Jr. (1981) has pointed out, the history of social studies has most frequently been used to invoke that part of the past that best justifies the actions of some individual or group in the present. That is not my intention. Rather, my theme is that NCSS grew out of a period of dissension regarding which groups should hold authority over social studies in the schools. This issue was, and remains, contested terrain. As I have argued elsewhere, although I do not find the periodic shrillness of these "turf battles" always productive, to a considerable extent they are inevitable (Thornton 1994). While curriculum decisions in all school subjects entail asking the question "What knowledge is of most worth?" in social studies the answer takes on special urgency: Who gets to define what the United States (as well as the rest of the world) has been, is, and should be?

Of course, it would be disingenuous to pretend that I bring no perspective of my own to this essay. Therefore, I assert my view at the outset that social studies reformers (both within and outside NCSS) have too often been preoccupied with promoting a particular subject (e.g., history, economics) or model of curriculum and/or instruction (e.g., inquiry, values clarification, issues centered), while giving too little weight to the proposition that good practice is possible in a variety of subjects and models (see, e.g., Brophy 1993). Reformers have repeatedly returned to the same or closely related arguments about what the social studies is (or are) and what it (or they) should be. Leadership on these and related questions, it was hoped, could be accomplished by founding NCSS.

Before NCSS

The closing decades of the nineteenth century and opening decades of the twentieth century were a period of modernization for the United States. Of particular relevance here was the rise of mass, taxpayer-funded public schooling. As the nation's public school population burgeoned, issues of public policy arose: What should be taught? How should instruction be organized? By what criteria should school programs be judged? Who should assume responsibility for teacher education? In earlier American history, the curriculum of any given classroom was largely determined by what the teacher knew and the content of whatever textbook might be available. Curriculum development as a professional undertaking or as a field of scholarly inquiry did not exist. By the turn of the century, however, Americans were engaged in what Robert Wiebe (1967) calls "the search for order." Increasingly, standardization rather than pluralism was coming to be valued in educational policy and practice. This process became a quest, as David Tyack (1974) puts it, for the "one best system" of schooling.

The search for order was also to affect what became the social studies in other ways. Coinciding with the rise of mass, public schooling was the founding of professional organizations in history and the social sciences such as the American Historical Association (AHA) in 1884 and the American Economic Association (AEA) in 1885. Thus, learned societies in what eventually became known as the "disciplines" were soon to join already established professional organizations such as the National Education Association (NEA) to claim a legitimate stake in the making of educational policy. Significantly, the priorities of these two types of professional organizations were not always in harmony. In time, both were to assert their right to the last word in the making of educational policy (Hertzberg 1981; Novick 1988).

Still, when the first major effort to forge some uniformity in what was taught in American secondary schools was made in 1893, the lines between the disciplinary organizations (and, indeed, the disciplines themselves) and professional groups remained relatively fluid. The notion of college- and university-based historians and social scientists as disciplinary specialists remained in its formative stages, and many people moved back and forth between jobs in higher education and jobs in the public school system (Thevenet 1994).

Nevertheless, at the beginning of the century, a process of bureaucratization was already well under way in American education. For example, there emerged regional history teachers' associations that brought together historians, social scientists, professors of education, and school people. Although relatively few teachers supported these regional organizations (Vanaria 1958, 84), teaching was becoming increasingly specialized, especially at the secondary level. The title of a 1919 article by David Snedden, a prominent proponent of educational efficiency—"The Professional Improvement of Teachers and Teaching through Organization"—is indicative of what many educational leaders saw as the wave of the future. Indeed, prior to NCSS, the National Council for Teachers of Mathematics and the National Council of Teachers of English had already been established (Murra 1970). Both the specialized "needs" of social studies teachers and what was seen as desirable standardization of the curriculum were to be used to justify the founding of NCSS.

Founding NCSS

A 1916 NEA report on secondary education is usually considered a turning point in the history of social studies. The motives and intentions of the authors of this report remain disputed (see Lybarger 1991; Saxe 1991; Whelan 1991). However, the report established a secondary school social studies scope and sequence that essentially has endured to the present day. The 1916 report's scope and sequence included courses in community civics, world history, and modern problems that had not previously been taught in some, probably most, secondary schools. The scope and sequence also included different approaches to traditional subjects such as American history. Circulation of the report resulted, as Louis Vanaria (1958) noted, in "chaos in school social studies programs" because school administrators and curriculum makers responded in diverse ways to the 1916 proposals (79). Although the 1916 report appears to have popularized the term "social studies," there was still little agreement on scope and sequence. About one-third of the schools followed older AHA recommendations, one-third the 1916 NEA recommendations, and the remainder various other curriculum schemes (Dawson 1929, 373).

At this time, many problems roiled the social studies field: disagreement on scope and sequence, insufficient guidance on defining the content of new courses such as communi-

ty civics, lack of certification requirements for teaching social studies, and little cooperation on teacher education between professors of education and professors of social studies subjects. The founders of NCSS believed that these problems would be best addressed by creating an organization to bring all the interested parties together (Murra 1970; Vanaria 1958). To this end, in 1920, a group from Teachers College, Columbia University decided to launch a movement. This decision resulted in a meeting in Atlantic City in 1921 at which NCSS was "founded."

Although NCSS was thus established to serve as "a central clearinghouse to coordinate the activity of groups in the social studies" (Vanaria 1958, 91), its founders and early leaders were not school teachers but rather college professors in both the social studies disciplines and education (Vanaria 1958, 119). Nonetheless, the first secretary of the fledgling organization, Edgar Dawson, was compelled from the outset to justify the name and purposes of NCSS because of suspicions and criticisms from some historians and social scientists. As early as 1922, Dawson wrote that

the use by the National Council of the term "social studies" did not arise from any prejudice in favor of a hash of all kinds of subject matter thrown together. ...The term...was adopted as the only one now available that distinguishes the social studies subjects from other parts of the school curriculum. (Vanaria 1958, 91)

For Dawson as well as for some recent observers (e.g., Jenness 1990), social studies signified little, if anything, more than a catch-all label: "Any title," Dawson continued, "which educators and scholars will agree on is good enough" (quoted in Vanaria 1958, 91).

What seems clear in retrospect is that, from its earliest days, NCSS brought together people with a variety of conceptions of what "social studies" means. Some hoped to see history and the social sciences unified for purposes of instruction, often centered on societal issues or "problems"; some preferred simply more coordination between efforts in the constituent subjects; and some wished to promote the teaching of a particular subject.

Even if Dawson's view truly represented the NCSS membership, however, social studies looked like a suspect and ill-defined entity to many historians and social scientists and, significantly, was sometimes perceived as a curricular rival (Lagemann 1992; Novick 1988). These criticisms have recurred even when seemingly impartial observers of the social studies such as David Jenness (1990) have emphasized that NCSS has tended to be an umbrella type organization incorporating a variety of perspectives, including considerable support for the teaching of the disciplines. This explanation, however, has never entirely stilled criticism from successive generations of historians and social scientists. Members of those groups have periodically charged that social studies is what Lawrence Cremin (1990) called "popular education," in which, it is said, the standards of the more traditional, college preparation liberal arts program are compromised.

At the outset, NCSS had enjoyed the support of AHA and NEA in a variety of ways. Nonetheless, within a generation after the founding of NCSS, collaboration between NCSS and disciplinary organizations such as AHA largely fell apart. There was a growing tendency, which has continued to this day, for the learned societies either to ignore NCSS or to see it as an obstacle rather than an ally in pursuit of broadly similar goals.

NCSS Finds Its Feet

Throughout the 1920s and well into the 1930s, NCSS carried out only a fraction of its current activities. While there was no real dispute that teachers of the social studies needed information concerning the current status of the social studies, new programs in progress throughout the country, the names of leaders in the development of these programs, sources of information and assistance, and professional resources (Hartshorn 1971, 518), only gradually did NCSS assemble the necessary means and independence to carry out its mission in ways that had any likelihood of being effectual on a national scale.

Indeed, in its first few years, most of the NCSS membership was concentrated in the northeastern industrial states, especially the New York City region (Vanaria 1958). The *Historical Outlook*, its journal at that time (Day 1987), was subsidized by AHA and was not even owned by NCSS. The first NCSS yearbooks, beginning in 1922, were published as part of the journal, not as separate publications, and NCSS did not hold an independent national meeting.

Although the 1930s began inauspiciously for NCSS, with falling membership accompanying the deepening of the Great Depression, NCSS finished the decade resembling today's organization in terms of functions and autonomy. In 1931, NCSS issued its first separate yearbook, which added to a mere four bulletins that had been the extent of its previous publishing efforts beyond its journal. The publication of a yearbook was one indicator of an emerging, more independent role for NCSS in social studies teaching, curriculum, and staff development. As the thirties wore on, more signs of this growing confidence and independence were to appear.

At the same time that NCSS was finding its organizational feet, AHA continued to maintain a leadership role in social studies. At the end of the 1920s, AHA established a Commission on Social Studies (which included prominent historians such as Charles A. Beard as well as four leaders of NCSS). This committee's findings were published in an ambitious series of books on the social studies that appeared in the early to mid thirties. It was perhaps a harbinger of things to come that the commission was characterized by deep disagreements among its members (including between Beard and some of the other, more traditional, historians) concerning appropriate goals for the social studies. In the end, no recommendations for scope and sequence were issued (Hertzberg 1981). By default, much of the task of interpreting the commission's recommendations for educational practice fell to discussion in forums such as NCSS publications.

The remainder of the 1930s saw a number of developments that enhanced the role of NCSS. In 1935, NCSS held its first annual meeting separate from AHA. In 1936, NCSS—with AHA's continued subsidy and sponsorship—at last acquired its own publication, *Social Education*. The first issue appeared in 1937 under the editorship of Professor Erling Hunt of Teachers College (Day 1987). Unlike earlier publications, *Social Education* would be identified with NCSS from the outset (Hertzberg 1981, 54). And, in 1940, NCSS appointed its first full-time executive secretary, Wilbur F. Murra, thus providing far greater administrative continuity and a permanent headquarters.

At the same time that NCSS was marshalling the means to disseminate its ideas, practitioners and curriculum leadership were coming more to the fore in the organization. The year 1939 saw for the first time a practicing school teacher, Ruth West, assume the NCSS presidency. In the same year, NCSS's "Curriculum Series" monographs were launched. As West made plain in her foreword to the first volume of this series (Michener 1939), NCSS was taking an initiative in two areas where the most recent AHA commission had not: scope and sequence. Nonetheless, West described NCSS's task as taking "practicable next steps" in the wake of the AHA commission, not rejecting it. Soon, however, underlying tensions between the learned societies and NCSS were to come very much into the open with, at least initially, historians and social studies educators cast not as collaborators but as enemies.

This dispute began at the height of World War II and concerned the results of a widely publicized test on American history administered to 7,000 college freshmen. The test results, published in the *New York Times*, were described as disgraceful, particularly at a time when the American heritage was imperiled. The cause of the low test scores, prominent American historian Allan Nevins charged, was that American history was being neglected in schools and colleges. Others soon joined Nevins in the attack, and charges were levelled that "social studies extremists" were to blame for Americans' supposedly woeful ignorance of the facts of their history. These attacks infuriated Hunt, who, in Hazel Hertzberg's words (1981), "proceeded to take apart the *Times* test" in the pages of *Social Education* (69).

Eventually, perceiving a common crisis as the dispute escalated, NCSS, AHA, and the Mississippi Valley Historical Association (now the Organization of American Historians) joined forces. They conducted a collaborative national study and issued a report, *American History in Schools and Colleges* (1944), in which Edgar Wesley, a former NCSS President, summarized the study's findings and recommendations. The report is still well worth reading and presents a remarkably balanced set of recommendations on the teaching of American history and related issues such as curriculum scope and sequence and teacher education. Significantly, although firmly refuting charges that American history was being neglected in schools and colleges, Wesley steered clear of the crisis mentality in which the whole affair had begun. All three organizations carried through, albeit to varying extents, with dissemination of the report's recommendations. The report remains a fine example of how the learned societies and NCSS could cooperate, each drawing on its particular strengths, to address—and, at least temporarily, largely settle at the scholarly level, if not in practice—a problem of mutual concern. As Hertzberg (1981) observed, however, "This joint effort on the teaching of American history may have halted for the moment the distancing between the 'professional historians' and social studies teaching in the schools, but the halt was only a brief one" (72).

The Legacy of NCSS's Early Years

As the Wesley report showed, NCSS by the 1940s was capable of acting as a peer rather than merely a junior partner with the learned societies. Since that time, however, collaboration among NCSS and the learned societies has been spasmodic and, not infrequently, contentious. For examples, refer to the largely hostile responses to the recent National Commission on Social Studies (jointly sponsored by AHA, the Carnegie Foundation for the Advancement of Teaching, NCSS, and OAH) in the November/December 1990 issue of *Social Education* (Epstein and Evans 1990).

In American higher education since World War II, the priorities of scholars in the social studies disciplines and those concerned with teaching social studies in schools have grown more distant. Historians and social scientists have tended increasingly to be preoccupied with their research specialties and, unlike the situation at the turn of the century, to hold professional identities that are usually distinct from those concerned with social studies teaching (Hertzberg 1980). AHA continued to subsidize NCSS until 1954, and its name continued on the cover of *Social Education* as late as 1968. However, historians, who almost always had taken a greater interest in the schools than their colleagues in the social sciences, now had few incentives, for example, to write synthesiz-

ing schoolbooks as earlier generations of historians had done (Hertzberg 1980, 497).

Nevertheless, as should be evident, the politics of knowledge have been present in social studies in some form from the very beginning. The battles we see today are not new. In this sense, we should not be entirely surprised that there are presently overlapping proposals for national standards in history, geography, and social studies. Perhaps less widely appreciated, however, is that "turf battles" are not only between NCSS and other organizations; they are also within NCSS. There have always been contrasting views of the field's proper goals within NCSS. For examples, we need look no further than three of the best-known figures of the early years of NCSS: Henry Johnson and Hunt strongly maintained that history should not be integrated into an interdisciplinary social studies, while Wesley favored a more fusionist position on the disciplines (Hertzberg 1981; Johnson 1940; Robinson 1985). In other words, skepticism is generally warranted when individuals claim to be speaking on behalf of the entire NCSS membership (Risinger 1991).

Finally, as Hertzberg was fond of pointing out, the social studies field has tended, ironically enough, to be ahistorical. Although historical perspective cannot tell us what to do in the present, it can surely lend perspective to the efforts of today's social studies educators. As William Faulkner (1975) wrote, "The past is never dead. It's not even past."

Acknowledgement

I am grateful to Ellen Condliffe Lagemann and Andrew D. Mullen for their critiques of an earlier version of this essay.

References

Brophy, J., ed. *Advances in Research on Teaching*. Vol. 4. *Case Studies of Teaching and Learning in*

Social Studies. Greenwich, Conn.: JAI Press, 1993.

Cremin, L. A. *Popular Education and Its Discontents.* New York: Harper & Row, 1990.

Davis, O. L., Jr. "Understanding the History of the Social Studies." In *The Social Studies,* edited by H. D. Mehlinger and O. L. Davis, Jr. Chicago: University of Chicago Press, 1981.

Dawson, Edgar. "Efforts toward Reorganization." *The Historical Outlook* 20, no. 8 (December 1929): 372-75.

Day, Billie. "A Brief History of *Social Education*" *Social Education* 51, no. 1 (January 1987): 10-15.

Epstein, T. L., and R. W. Evans, eds. "Reactions to *Charting a Course.*" Special Section in *Social Education,* 54, no. 7 (November/December 1990): 427-46.

Faulkner, William. "Intruder in the Dust." In *Requiem for a Nun.* New York: Vintage, 1975.

Hartshorn, M. F. "National Council for the Social Studies." In *The Encyclopedia of Education,* edited by L. C. Deighton. n.p.: Macmillan, 1971.

Hertzberg, H. W. "The Teaching of History." In *The Past Before Us: Contemporary Historical Writing in the United States,* edited by M. Kammen. Ithaca, N.Y.: Cornell University Press, 1980.

———. *Social Studies Reform, 1880-1980.* Boulder, Colo: Social Science Education Consortium, 1981.

Jenness, D. *Making Sense of Social Studies.* New York: Macmillan, 1990.

Johnson, H. *Teaching of History in Elementary and Secondary Schools with Applications to Allied Studies.* rev. ed. New York: Macmillan, 1940.

Lagemann, E. C. *The Politics of Knowledge: The Carnegie Corporation, Philanthropy, and Public Policy.* Middletown, Conn.: Wesleyan University Press, 1989.

———. "Prophecy or Profession? George S. Counts and the Social Study of Education." *American Journal of Education* 100 (1992): 137-65.

Lybarger, M. B. "The Historiography of Social Studies: Retrospect, Circumspect, and Prospect." In *Handbook of Research on Social Studies Teaching and Learning,* edited by J. P. Shaver. New York: Macmillan, 1991.

Michener, James A. *The Future of the Social Studies:*

Proposals for an Experimental Social Studies Curriculum. Cambridge, Mass.: National Council for the Social Studies, 1939.

Murra, W. F. "The Birth of NCSS—As Remembered by Earl U. Rugg." *Social Education* 34 (1970): 728-29.

Novick, P. *That Noble Dream: The 'Objectivity Question' and the American Historical Profession.* Cambridge, England: Cambridge University Press, 1988.

Risinger, C. Frederick. "Unkept Promises and New Opportunities: Social Studies Education and the New World Order." *Social Education* 55, no. 2 (February 1991): 138-41.

Robinson, P. "Henry Johnson and the Place of History in Education for World Peace." *Social Education* 49, no. 2 (February 1985): 160-62.

Saxe, D. W. *Social Studies in Schools: A History of the Early Years.* Albany, N.Y.: State University of New York Press, 1991.

Thevenet, P. C. "The Beginnings of Standardized Social Studies Curriculum in the Elementary Schools." Ph.D. diss., Columbia University, 1994.

Thornton, S. J. "The Social Studies Near Century's End: Reconsidering Patterns of Curriculum and Instruction." In *Review of Research in Education* 20, edited by L. Darling-Hammond. Washington, D.C.: American Educational Research Association, 1994.

Tyack, D. B. *The One Best System: A History of American Urban Education.* Cambridge, Mass.: Harvard University Press, 1974.

Vanaria, L. M. "The National Council for the Social Studies: A Voluntary Organization for Professional Service." Ph.D. diss., Columbia University, 1958.

Wesley, E. B. *American History in Schools and Colleges.* New York: Macmillan, 1944.

Whelan, M. "James Harvey Robinson, the New History, and the 1916 Social Studies Report." *History Teacher* 24 (1991): 191-202.

Wiebe, R. H. *The Search for Order, 1877-1920.* New York: Hill and Wang, 1967.

NCSS *and the Nature of Social Studies*

James L. Barth
Purdue University

THE "NATURE" OF SOMETHING IS USUALLY UNDERSTOOD TO MEAN ITS essence, or the intrinsic identity that sets it apart and gives it a unique quality. For instance, the essence of teaching, according to Dreeben in *The Nature of Teaching* (1970, 1), is to "effect changes in people." According to Homans, the social sciences also have an essential nature: "They share the same subject matter—the behavior of men. And they employ ... the same body of general explanatory principles" (1967, 3).

The nature of the social studies is somewhat different in emphasis from the behavioral focus of the social sciences, though it complements the essence of teaching, namely, "to effect changes in people." Educators have been developing positions on and analyzing the nature of the social studies for the past seventy-five years. This chapter surveys the long-standing debate over the nature of the social studies and explores the implications of that debate for curriculum and practice.

Identifying a Nature of the Social Studies

One well-known social studies theorist, Edgar Bruce Wesley, began by defining the essential area of learning in each part of the school curriculum. Thus, the study of quantification is assigned to mathematics, communication to English, leisure to recreation, work to vocation, location to geography, and relationships to social studies. This was his description of the essence of social studies:

> *The heart of the social studies is relationships—relationships primarily between and among human beings . . . but the single person does not constitute the major concern of the studies until*

he establishes a network of relationships with at least one other person. Naturally he also joins groups, organizations, institutions and in turn these create a seamless web of human relations. They constitute the heart and essence of the social studies. (Barr, Barth, and Shermis 1978, iv, v)

In Wesley's view, and generally in the view of members of the National Council for the Social Studies (NCSS), the pre-K through 12 school curriculum assigns the examination of the "seamless web of human relations" to social studies, and those relations then mature in the context of "a culturally diverse, democratic society in an interdependent world" (NCSS 1992). Those who agree posit that an integrated social studies curriculum actually has as its content all human experience that bears upon the role of citizen. They define social studies as "an integration of experience and knowledge concerning human relations for the purpose of citizenship education" (Barr, Barth, and Shermis 1977, 69).

From this perspective, human relations are to be viewed as maturing within the context of multiple levels of citizenship ranging from family to school to community to state to nation and all the way to global citizenship. The maturing of these different levels of citizenship, according to the founders and proponents of the social studies field, should not be left to chance, politicians, or the implied benefit of a general education; rather, it should be the concern of trained social studies teachers who follow an integrated social studies curriculum. The field, then, is monitored in a school curriculum designed to examine citizenship relationships as reflected in human experience. This examination of human relations is the first critical element that defines the unique nature of social studies.

In an integrated social studies curriculum, the social sciences, humanities, and other areas of study offer the facts, concepts, and general-izations that constitute the content. However, the relevance of the content is measured by its application to the problems and issues of citizens. Shirley Engle would insist that critical evaluation accompanied by decision making is the purpose for integrating the content and thus should be practiced in the classroom throughout a social studies curriculum (Engle 1963, 306; 1960, 196). For example, sociology would examine family and community relations, history would examine relations in the past, economics would examine material relations, political science would examine government relations, geography would examine location relations, anthropology would examine the origin and development of humankind, humanities would examine human attributes, and critical-social problems would be examined by any subject area that could provide information about those problems (Wesley and Wronski 1964, 2).

Although discrete areas of study can be identified as noted here, it is not to be assumed that the issues of citizenship are necessarily the exclusive domain of any social science or history area. In fact, the study of human relations requires the integration of all areas that reflect upon the problem. Thus, a second critical element that defines the unique nature of social studies is the integrating of the social sciences, humanities, and other areas of study for the purpose of examining all human relation experiences among citizens.

Some Deny the Nature and Existence of the Social Studies

Not all who acknowledge social studies as a school curriculum area believe, with Wesley and others, that the field necessarily has a unique quality or intrinsic identity that would suggest a nature of the social studies. For some, there may be a curriculum area, but not necessarily a nature.

In fact, there are those who do not consider

education and, in particular, social studies, a professional activity. They think of education as only a theory of instruction, perhaps a curriculum organization or an application of the art of teaching, without an intrinsic identity. In this view, social studies has no real nature because it has no identity such as "a unique set of laws and principles and a unique mode of inquiry" (Nelson 1991, 44) that sets it apart from the social sciences and humanities. Correspondingly, citizenship education, for some, is assigned to the entire school, to education in general. They argue that all good education teaches the fundamentals of the good life. Thus, citizenship practice and principles are not necessarily confined in a school curriculum to the area of social studies.

Others would argue that social studies is a myth because it has rarely been practiced as a K-12 school curriculum. In this view, social studies teachers consider themselves practitioners of one or more of the social sciences or of history. They do not intend to integrate their particular discipline with history or other social science disciplines or to integrate it into the school social studies scope and sequence. In practical terms, teaching about all human relations, including the study of issues and problems, is filtered through history or some other discrete discipline, and social studies is merely a label for a school curriculum area.

Clair Keller, an advocate of a history-centered curriculum, represents some of these arguments and adds to them:

> It is time to put the debate to rest and abandon the myth that social studies exists as a discipline . . . for in reality it has never existed, does not exist, and will not exist in the classroom. It exists only in the minds of social studies disciples. Although teachers have always been willing to use the term social studies as an adjective describing the area they teach, they seldom use it as a noun to describe what they teach. (1991, 69)

Keller contends that among those who do not see an essence of social studies, the only real debate is about how to teach the individual social sciences and history. To take his position to its logical conclusion, the National Council for the Social Studies would be renamed the National Council for Teachers of History and Social Science, and social studies departments in schools and universities would be renamed departments of social science education. The effect of Keller's position would be to associate social science education with the goals of liberal arts and the purpose of informed citizens, thus eliminating the social studies, which is associated with a social mission and a methodology that includes "knowledge concerning human relations for the purpose of citizenship education" (Barr, Barth, and Shermis 1977, 69). Even the NCSS charter in 1921 stated, "The term social studies ... is used to include history, economics, sociology, civics, geography, and all modifications of subjects whose content as well as aim is social" (Barr, Barth, and Shermis 1977, 2).

Given this charter, if the field of social studies is no more than the social sciences simplified for pedagogical purposes, as Wesley maintained, then social studies is just the name of a curricular cluster that has no critical elements, no intrinsic identity. Commenting on the argument for the study of separate social science and history subjects in the schools, Wilma Longstreet concludes: "To the extent that the real curriculum of the social studies means history, there is clearly no need for a discipline of the social studies" (1991, 26).

Social Studies Does Exist, Others Say, but Disagree about Its Nature and Practice

As we have seen from Wesley's web of relations and Engle's insistence on decision making, some have identified a nature of the social studies but disagree about its critical elements. They also debate the application of that nature to instruction in a social studies curriculum.

A review of how some social studies proponents have thought about the critical elements that make up the social studies will illustrate this debate. Longstreet, for example, sees social studies as an education program to prepare citizens for participation in a democratic society. She asks the question, "Can a discipline be developed based on the social studies?" (1991, 27). She answers by saying, "What appears to be lacking is not a discipline of the social studies but rather a discipline of citizenship" (1991, 29). She reasons,

> *Unless we succeed in developing some basic knowledge about the nature of citizenship, its different functions, how these functions interact with one another, how personal life and citizenship life function separately and interactively, social studies objectives involving the development of citizenship are likely to remain unaccomplished.* (1991, 31)

Another educator, O. L. Davis, Jr., disagrees. For Davis, "Citizenship education fails as the central justification of the social studies in American schools and burdens this curricular area because the term is a dead metaphor" (1991, 33). Davis points out that social studies in its inception some eighty years ago and during its early development showed signs of maturing into a concern for citizenship education. However, during its middle and late years, citizenship education as the purpose of social studies has become "burdensome" and "a downright liability" (1991, 33).

Although there are multiple reasons for this liability, teaching social studies has become just a "technical aspect of citizenship" (Davis 1991, 35). In short,

> *social studies subjects are taught lifelessly. They are routinely dull . . . bland stories, vague explanations, maybe some old photographs and decaying documents, and of*

> *course facts and maps. This part of the social studies has [nothing] viable to contribute to students' understanding of an heightened interest in active engagements in the common, civic life of their society.* (1991, 35)

He concludes that citizenship education, if it were properly revived in the future, could once more be the central justification for social studies. Although both Longstreet and Davis are attacking social studies education as practiced, they both focus on citizenship education as the intrinsic identity, the unique quality that will revive social studies.

Most commentators agree that true, comprehensive social studies have yet to be implemented in the schools. Keller speaks of a myth. Davis identifies citizenship education as a dead metaphor. D. W. Saxe states bluntly, "The problem is social studies is not currently offered in schools" (1992, 17). Some would argue that the schools, with the exception of a few that were experimental, have never yet actually offered an integrated pre-K through 12 social studies program. Lawrence Metcalf provided the classic comment when asked, "Whatever happened to social studies?" by responding, "Social studies did not fail, it was never tried" (Saxe 1992, 17). Some critics would respond by asking, How can the challenge of practice be met if the nature of the social studies is still unclear and evolving?

What Is Basic to the Social Studies?

Without attempting here to reconcile the various debates over the nature of the social studies, I think it is at least possible to define its essential elements. First, education is often defined as change, but the meaning of change in social studies education has been refined to include improving the welfare of citizens. Second, the social studies is based on an instructional methodology that assumes the curriculum will meet the developing needs and interests of students. Meeting those needs involves identifying problems and issues that should be examined through a reflective inquiry process. Third, the development of democratic citizens is both a social and an educational mission of social studies instruction. These elements were not clearly perceived during the early development of social studies; rather, they have evolved throughout the twentieth century. But to understand that evolution as a study of a "seamless web of human relationships," we must start by asking, Why social studies? Where did it come from?

Social Studies and Citizenship Education

Citizenship education existed in the eighteenth and nineteenth centuries, but that education was not synonymous with social studies. Some social studies proponents have argued that not only was the notion of social studies an outgrowth of progressive education theory but that it also has roots in the populist movement, particularly those roots that emphasized democracy and participation in the political process.

Imagine a tree with a trunk labeled citizenship education and four branches that have grown from that trunk. The first branch and the oldest of the traditional ways of teaching citizenship education was patriotic history in the nineteenth century, which was intended to inculcate moral beliefs. The second branch grew out of the recommendations of two committees, the 1893 National Education Association (NEA) Committee of Ten and the 1899 American Historical Association (AHA) Committee of Seven. These committees recommended a reform of patriotic history by studying events through an "analytical scientific approach" intended to be a strong academic secondary school program. The third branch, based on a committee recommendation from the 1905 AHA Committee of Eight, offered an alternative to the two earlier committees' recommendations. The 1905 AHA Committee stated that "history [as classical ideas and ideals] was … prerequisite to effective democratic citizenship" (Barr, Barth, and Shermis 1977, 19). The committee's point was that the teaching of history had a mission beyond being scientific; it also had to foster democratic citizenship. The fourth branch, social studies, also sought to reform nineteenth-century citizenship education, which social studies advocates believed had much to do with inculcating patriotism but little to do with developing thoughtful, decision-making citizens in a democratic society.

In many ways, the "muckrakers" and other social critics at the turn of the century, with their attention to social welfare, social reform, social efficiency, and the development of democratic citizens, set the agenda from which social studies would emerge as a school subject in the 1920s (Hertzberg 1981, 17). Those social critics—such as Ida Tarbell, Sinclair Lewis, John Dewey, and Jane Addams—shared the view that twentieth-century America would experience rapid change dominated by technology and interdependence and that the traditional family and community would have a decreasing influence on values and beliefs. Where, they asked, would discussion about citizens' values and beliefs and their consequences, social/personal problems and issues, and the practice of democracy take place in the society? They argued that such discussions would not be encouraged by citizenship education that taught moral lessons from McGuffey's Readers or patriotic history because both are based on indoctrination, which discourages the practice of reflective decision making. Surely, social critics also said, the second and third branches—the scientific history, geography, and civics suggested by the 1893, 1899, and 1905 committees—would not generate discussion on problems of democracy either.

The fourth branch, social studies, was formally suggested by the 1916 NEA Commission on the Reorganization of Secondary Education—Committee on the Social Studies. Advocates of social studies agreed with the social critics' predictions of deteriorating family relations, loss of community identity, and the abuse of democratic institutions. But these advocates turned to the school as the best hope of preparing effective citizens by having students practice democratic traditions throughout a K-12 social studies curriculum. In this way, the responsibility for considering values and beliefs and identifying the meanings and practices of a democratic way of life shifted from parents to the school. That responsibility gave the school an additional mission beyond the three Rs but not a clear mandate on just how the mission should be carried out in a diverse, democratic society.

Of the four competing views outlined here, which is most effective in preparing citizens for twentieth-century democratic society? Which branch of the citizenship education tree should be nurtured and encouraged to grow and which should be pruned?

There is little consensus among parents, administrators, social studies teachers, and university professors on the answers to these questions. In fact, all four competing views may be found in most school social studies programs. Why has social studies, the fourth branch, not emerged as the appropriate answer to the citizenship question?

Jack Nelson offers two hypotheses (1991, 45). He argues that if social studies had become a field in the latter part of the nineteenth century and then emerged at the same time as the social sciences in the early twentieth century, it would now have the status of a discipline. Unfortunately, in his view, the theory and organization that would support social studies instruction did not emerge until after both history and the social sciences had already become professionally established.

Thus, social studies has always been filtered through a variety of lenses: patriotic moral lessons, the history profession, the social science profession, and the recommendations of the 1916 Committee on the Social Studies, which even today continues to exercise some influence over curriculum organization and methodology.

The founders of the social studies, according to Nelson's other hypothesis, in the second and third decades of the twentieth century, failed to commit themselves to a field with a unique nature of its own, preferring to accept the role of social studies as simplified social science and history for use in the schools. In short, the field was merely a conduit for the already established social sciences and history. Thus, social studies began its maturing in the public mind as merely an adjunct of history and social sciences—having no identity itself and useful only as a means of describing a cluster of discrete courses. This impression, of course, was reinforced by the 1921 NCSS charter, which stated, "The social studies is conceived as the subject matter of the academic disciplines, somehow 'simplified,' 'adapted,' 'modified,' or selected for school instruction" (Barr, Barth, and Shermis 1977, 2).

NCSS and the Nature of the Social Studies

"From History to Social Studies" is how Hazel Hertzberg (1981, 17) summarizes what would become one of the persistent arguments within NCSS. Throughout the seventy-five years of NCSS's existence, members have often debated the meaning of social studies as citizenship education and the role of NCSS in defining the nature of the social studies. Three general perspectives have dominated: (1) social studies should mean the teaching of history; (2) social studies should reflect its populist and progressive roots but should have as its core the teaching of scientific/analytical history supplemented by the various social sciences; and (3) social studies should recognize its populist and progressive roots but emphasize the education of democratic citizens through an integration of content that centers on social/personal problems and issues as studied in a reflective process.

Throughout the history of NCSS, these perspectives have revolved in and out of favor as educational reforms. Usually, the perspective in favor mirrors the political mood of the country at that time, with certain arguments finding support during more liberal periods.

The cyclical character of these perspectives has created monumental challenges for educators who must translate theory into practice. One of the tasks of NCSS over its history has been to help translate the nature of the social studies into operational statements. But, in addition to the challenge of developing implementation plans for an evolving process, the task has been made even more difficult because of the persistent arguments about NCSS's role in defining the meaning of social studies as citizenship education.

In the 1920s, NCSS associated itself with the American Historical Association (AHA). The founders of the social studies, as well as many of NCSS's subsequent leaders, had a history bias, and as we have already seen, the NCSS charter reflected that bias while accepting progressive education focused on history as the core of social studies content.

In the latter part of the 1920s, Harold Rugg, a so-called "reconstructionist" educator, introduced a social studies curriculum based on an integration of content that focused on social problems. His action was an attempt to implement and extend the 1916 Commission recommendations. Also in the latter part of the 1920s, AHA organized a Commission on the Social Studies that lasted into the mid-1930s. Clearly, this commission can be seen as an advocate for history as the core of social studies content, with the social sciences supple-

menting that core. This commission's argument recycled the 1905 Committee of Eight recommendation, updated in the 1930s. Specifically, the AHA committee found the course on the problems of democracy recommended by the 1916 Committee on the Social Studies to be insufficient, as were Rugg's reconstructionist ideas. It viewed both as too closely related to the argument that the study of contemporary social/person problems should be undertaken through an inquiry process.

It was clear by the mid-1930s that there were those in NCSS who would argue for "the loose constructionist version of education for citizenship" (Hertzberg 1981, 39). In this view, NCSS was to be an umbrella organization that welcomed all points of view but had little philosophical structure and no pretense of helping social studies become a disciplinary field. Because NCSS did not provide an official definition of social studies, curriculum standards, or any statement on recommended ways to view teaching and learning, anything could fit within the category of social studies. Nevertheless, even then, some in NCSS were looking to define an intrinsic identity that would set social studies apart and thus make it a distinct disciplinary field.

In 1935, under the leadership of Edgar Wesley, NCSS separated from AHA and held its own annual convention. At this time, historians took less interest than before in NCSS and the teaching of social studies. These developments were triggered in part by the twentieth-century movement toward specialization. Social studies, history, and the social sciences were all tending to become specialized. However, despite increasing pressure for specialization, NCSS continued to support a loose construction, umbrella-organization approach, and no official attempts were made to define social studies for another sixty years.

NCSS, after separating from AHA, made some effort in the latter part of the 1930s to provide direction for the future of social studies. That effort took the form of offering suggestions on curriculum organization and scope and sequence. These suggestions, in line with John Dewey's ideas, were associated with reforms suggested by the 1916 Committee, Rugg in the 1920s, and the Progressive Education Association in the 1930s and 1940s. This was also the period of the Eight-Year Study focusing on experimental schools, in which different integrated versions of curriculums with a social studies core were tested.

In the 1940s, American youth were found to be deficient in basic information about their country. The same deficiency was found in the early 1950s and mid-1980s. On each occasion, a new interest was triggered in the question, What is an appropriate citizenship education? Most of that interest was driven by a conservative mood.

In the 1940s, the Committee on American History in the Schools and Colleges found that students lacked appropriate information. One of the committee's recommendations was that American history should be taught at the fifth-grade, eighth-grade, and high school levels, a three-course cycle that continues to be generally followed today.

Meanwhile, in its mid-1940s publications, NCSS began to take notice of global/international citizenship obligations, and take an interest in human relations emphasizing cultural pluralism and multicultural education. This attention tended to be supported by arguments favoring integration and the study of problems and issues gaining popularity at the time. This period also was an experimental time, when the Detroit and Columbia University citizenship education projects encouraged students to learn citizenship by doing, an obvious attempt to apply Dewey's notion of progressive education to the practice of social studies.

By the mid-1950s, Hunt and Metcalf had published their methods book, *Teaching High School Social Studies*. This text argued for the study of social problems through a reflective process, an argument closely related to Dewey and progressive education reforms. For more than a decade, this book remained the most influential methods text in the country and provided inspiration for reforms that would emerge in the 1970s.

A competing point of view in the 1950s, based on the discovery once again that students were deficient in basic information about their country, was articulated by Arthur Bestor, a principal critic of social studies. Bestor found social studies "soft," if not unintellectual. As a leader of a basic education movement, he advocated that social studies become history, a recycled argument from the early twentieth century.

However, by this time, the social sciences had begun to take an interest in citizenship education. Social scientists, with the assistance of NCSS, other professional associations, and government agencies such as the National Science Foundation, used Bruner's notion of "structures of the discipline" to propose a "New Social Studies." The idea was that each social science discipline, working through its professional organization, would propose its own version of how its structure was to be taught in the schools. In many ways, this reform was also a recycling of earlier proposals from the 1920s and 1930s.

By the latter part of the New Social Studies era (the late 1960s and the early 1970s), another reform began to take shape as the so-called "second phase" of the New Social Studies emerged. Social studies educators who favored progressive education turned the New Social Studies toward the "new" New Social Studies. This second phase was, in reality, merely a recycling of the same arguments for integration made between the time of the 1916 Commission and the appearance of Hunt and Metcalf's methods book in the 1950s. This second phase of the reform featured the reflective inquiry tradition, which was based less on intellectual structures of academic disciplines in social science and history and more on relevance to individual needs and interests and critical social problems set in problem-solving situations. Another reform in the late 1970s was a resurgence of the basic education movement, which argued for history as the proper medium of instruction for citizenship education.

In the 1980s, students were again discovered to have learned inadequately about their country. This time, given the conservative mood of the country, the answer was to emphasize the basics, history and geography, as proposed by the federal initiative called "America 2000." Social studies under this initiative would be essentially abandoned and replaced by a K-12 history and geography curriculum supported by federal standards and enforced by national testing. Chester Finn, speaking for this initiative, called social studies "a field that has been getting slimier and more tangled ever since it changed its name from 'history' around 1916." He continued,

> Even as social studies has become a grab bag of current events, … one-worldism, and opinion-mongering by uninformed children and half-informed adults [social studies teachers], it has not played a very large role in the education of young Americans. (1988, 16)

In the late 1980s, NCSS responded to the Finn argument by sponsoring, along with AHA, the National Geographic Society, and other professional organizations, a National Commission on the Social Studies in the Schools. The recommendation from this commission, published as *Charting a Course*, was to retain social studies, but to restructure it to emphasize history and geography and to include where appropriate other social sciences. *Charting a Course* was actually a reaffirmation of the argument for progressive education, but retained history and social

science as separate subjects, in a manner reminiscent of the 1905 Committee of Eight recommendation brought up to 1980s standards.

Following the issue of this report in 1989, the NCSS Board of Directors sought between 1992 and 1994 to identify for NCSS a mission statement, definition, standards, and statement on teaching and learning. This effort represented a reversal of policy about the role of NCSS, which had for seventy-one years supported a loose confederation of competing interests but had taken no official stand on the nature of the social studies. With this reversal, NCSS supported the argument that a nature of the social studies had emerged that could be defined and applied as standards and statements on teaching and learning. Clearly, the Board's effort at reform was to promote the argument for an integrated content based on students' needs and interests, all of which should be examined through a reflective process.

NCSS Takes a Stand

The cycling in and out of the three persistent perspectives on citizenship education has not been resolved, but for the first time, NCSS as an organization has taken a stand. That official stand is found in the following statements issued by the Board of Directors between 1992 and 1994. NCSS identifies its mission as

> *engaging and supporting educators in strengthening and advocating social studies.* (NCSS 1992)

As part of that mission, NCSS has attempted to summarize the critical elements, the essence, of social studies by adopting the following definition:

> *Social studies is the integration of the social sciences and humanities to promote civic competence.*

However, this definition requires a context that explains the meaning of "integration" and "civic competence." Thus, the definition continues with the following:

Within the school program, social studies provides coordinated, systematic study drawing upon such disciplines as anthropology, archaeology, economics, geography, history, law, philosophy, political science, psychology, religion, and sociology, as well as appropriate content from the humanities, mathematics, and natural sciences. The primary purpose of social studies is to help young people develop the ability to make informed and reasoned decisions for the public good as citizens of a culturally diverse, democratic society in an interdependent world. (NCSS 1992)

Although this definition sets social studies apart and assigns it a unique quality, the definition does not offer a context in which social studies is to be taught and learned. The following position statement provides a vision of teaching and learning that describes the forms of teacher-student interaction on the activities and materials that can most effectively promote citizenship education:

Recognizing that teacher-student interaction is the heart of education, the position statement offers guiding principles portraying ideal social studies teaching and learning. [It also] focuses on what constitutes powerful teaching and learning within a unified social studies curriculum, and not on how much emphasis each content area should receive ... Powerful social studies teaching helps students develop social understanding and civic efficacy. Social understanding is integrated knowledge of social aspects of the human condition.... Civic efficacy is the readiness and willingness to assume citizenship responsibilities. (NCSS 1993, 213)

Expectations of Excellence: Curriculum Standards for Social Studies provides an additional dimension to the interpretation of social studies beyond the definition and the position statement on teaching and learning. The standards propose a level of attainment, a measure of comparison, and a core of content that is basic to a school social studies curriculum.

Two main characteristics, ... distinguish social studies as a field of study: it is designed to promote civic competence; and it is integrative, incorporating many fields of endeavor. In specific and more detailed terms, these distinctions mean the following:

... Because schools and teachers cannot teach everything and because students cannot learn all there is to know, this document focuses on three purposes for these standards. The social studies standards should:
1. serve as a framework for K-12 social studies program design through the use of ten thematic strands;
2. serve as a guide for curriculum decisions by providing performance expectations regarding knowledge, processes, and attitudes essential for all students; and
3. provide examples of classroom practice to guide teachers in designing instruction to help students meet performance expectations. These social studies standards provide criteria for making decisions as curriculum planners and teachers address such issues as why teach social studies, what to include in the curriculum, how to teach it well to all students, and how to assess whether or not students are able to apply what they have learned. (NCSS 1994, 3, 13)

It is within this context that these social studies standards were created. They pay attention to the specific contributions of history, the social sciences, humanities, fine arts, the natural sciences, and other disciplines, while simultaneously providing an umbrella for the integrative potential of these several disciplines. This characteristic is the nature and strength of social studies; recognizing the importance of the disciplines and their specific perspectives in understanding topics, issues, and problems, but also recognizing that topics, issues, and problems transcend the boundaries of single disciplines and demand the power of integration within and across them. (NCSS 1994, 5)

Although the publication of these documents is not expected to resolve the debate over the nature of the social studies, NCSS has now clearly articulated its own position.

References

Barr, R. D., J. L. Barth, and S. S. Shermis. *Defining the Social Studies.* Bulletin 51. Washington, D.C.: National Council for the Social Studies, 1977.

Barr, R. D., J. L. Barth, and S. S. Shermis. *The Nature of the Social Studies.* Palm Springs, Calif.: ETC Publications, 1978.

Davis, O. L., Jr. "Citizenship Education as the Central Purpose of the Social Studies: The Heavy Load of a Dead Metaphor." *Social Studies as a Discipline.* Special issue of *The International Journal of Social Education 6* (1991): 33-36

Dreeben, R. *The Nature of Teaching.* Glenville, Ill.: Scott, Foresman and Company, 1970.

Engle, S. H. "Decision-Making: The Heart of the Social Studies." *Social Education 24* (1960): 306.

Engle, S. H. "Thoughts in Regard to Revision." *Social Education 27* (1963): 196.

Finn, C. E., "The Social Studies Debacle among the Educationaloids." *The American Spectator* (May 1988): 15-16.

Hertzberg, H. W. *Social Studies Reform, 1880-1980. A Project Span Report.* Boulder, Colo.: Social Studies Education Consortium, 1981.

Homans, G. C. *The Nature of Social Science.*

New York: Harcourt, Brace & World, 1967.

Keller, C. "It Is Time to Abolish the Mythology that the Social Studies Constitute a Discipline." *Social Studies as a Discipline.* Special issue of *The International Journal of Social Education 6* (1991): 69-75.

Longstreet, W. "Reflections on a Discipline of the Social Studies." *Social Studies as a Discipline.* Special issue of *The International Journal of Social Education 6* (1991): 25-32.

National Council for the Social Studies. *Definition and Mission Statement,* ratified by House of Delegates, NCSS Annual Meeting, Detroit, Mich., November 23, 1992.

National Council for the Social Studies. "A Vision of Powerful Teaching and Learning in the Social Studies: Building Social Understanding and Civic Efficacy. Task Force on Standards for Teaching and Learning in the Social Studies." *Social Education 57* (1993): 213.

National Council for the Social Studies. *Expectations of Excellence: Curriculum Standards for Social Studies.* Bulletin 89. Washington, D.C.: National Council for the Social Studies, 1994.

Nelson, Jack. "Discipline, Knowledge and Social Education." Social Studies as a Discipline. Special issue of *The International Journal of Social Education 6* (1991): 41-50.

Saxe, David W. "A History for Social Studies: A Prologue to Reformation." Inquiry in Social Studies: Curriculum, Research and Instruction. Special issue of *The Journal of the North Carolina Council for the Social Studies 20* (1992): 13-25.

Wesley, E. B., and S. P. Wronski. *Teaching Social Studies in High Schools.* 5th ed. Boston: D. C. Heath and Company, 1964.

NCSS *and the Teaching of History*

Linda S. Levstik
University of Kentucky

Even in a democracy, history always involves power and exclusion, for any history is always someone's history, told by that someone from a partial point of view. (Appleby, Hunt, and Jacob 1994, 11)

INTEREST IN HISTORY EDUCATION IS ROOTED IN FUNDAMENTAL QUESTIONS about what we can and should tell children and young adults about who they are, what place they have in the world, and how the world came to be the way it is. As Appleby, Hunt, and Jacob (1994) note, however, history is never either a neutral force or a complete worldview; history is always someone's history. It is little wonder, then, that educators have argued about whose history appears in the curriculum and how that history is presented. Although this debate did not originate with the National Council for the Social Studies (NCSS), it has certainly been at the center of a number of the ideological storms that have blown through the organization over the past seventy-five years.

The sometimes uneasy alliance between "history" and "social studies" in NCSS should not be surprising. One of the hallmarks of NCSS has been the amorphousness of its self-definition.[1] It has been, in many ways, an umbrella organization that shelters quite disparate points of view about the nature and purposes of history and the social sciences. Beyond that, however, some of the friction between history education and NCSS is a direct result of the circumstances surrounding the founding of the organization. NCSS was the product of two social phenomena. The first was the move toward professionalism among historians and a concomitant interest in how history was taught in the schools. The second was a growing interest among social scientists and social welfare advocates in an integrated field—often called "social studies"—aimed at social improvement and civic responsibility (Saxe 1992).

Roots of Dissension

By the second half of the nineteenth century, history and the social sciences were only hazily defined either as disciplines or professions (Hertzberg 1981; Novick 1988). As historians finally began to define themselves as professionals, they sought to craft a "scientific" discipline supported by "historical method"—reliance on primary sources, testing and weighing evidence—and producing historical narratives that attempted to tell "what really happened." In 1884 they also established the first professional society of historians, the American Historical Association (AHA). Within four years of its founding, AHA issued the first of a series of reports focusing on the place of history in the schools and making specific suggestions for the inclusion of disciplinary history in the curriculum. In doing so, the history profession sought further to clarify its status as disciplinary "gatekeeper" maintaining the separation between professional historians and "educationists" who were necessarily historical amateurs (Lubove 1965; Novick 1988). At the turn of the century, educators seemed to accept both the curricular suggestions and the status separation. Thus, by the time NCSS was founded in 1921, a clear link between the history profession and precollegiate schooling had already been established.

At about the same time that historians were establishing themselves as a separate and scientific discipline, social welfare advocates began arguing for an integrated field whose aim was social betterment (Saxe 1992). The term "social studies" was sometimes linked to this movement, and generally described an integration of such areas as sociology, economics, vocational guidance, and civics. Its aim was to help citizens better understand and solve contemporary problems (Saxe 1992; Lybarger 1991). Social studies conceived in this form did not always exclude history, but it certainly called for history focused on the present—an understanding of the immediate concerns of individuals and communities—rather than disciplinary history for its own sake (Lybarger 1991).

These two social movements converged, to some extent, in the "new history" of the early twentieth century. In 1912, James Harvey Robinson argued for a history that would illumine the present, investigate the conditions of everyday life, and be committed to social progress, social science, and education. His efforts helped pave the way for the inclusion of history in a social studies organization with social welfare aims. By 1916, then, when the report of the Committee on Social Studies appeared, history was generally considered part of the social studies (Tryon 1934; Lybarger 1991).

Certainly there were those who did not see a place for history in social studies, as well as those who saw a place only for history. David Snedden (1924), an educator, argued for history as "a handmaid to the study of the social environment of the child...." In response to similar arguments, Henry Johnson, a historian, argued that a social studies curriculum based on student interests and needs violated the integrity of history as a discipline (Lybarger 1991). Johnson's stance reflected the fear that social studies represented an academic "shortcut" that would bypass disciplinary history. On the other hand, Snedden's emphasis on present needs reflected the social welfare concern with civic education, and to some extent, that of the "new history" as well.

In the midst of these tensions, AHA supported the establishment of NCSS. The two organizations met jointly for some time, sharing responsibility for *The Historical Outlook*, the periodical that became *The Social Studies* and was the principal NCSS membership journal for a brief period until *Social Education* was launched. AHA continued to subsidize *Social Education* in its early years. At the same time, NCSS drew significant strength from the social welfare commitment to civic responsibility. The statement of purpose of the new national council, "education for citizenship through social studies," forthrightly aligned NCSS with the social welfare perspective (Lybarger 1991, 6). As a result, history was generally seen as a component of citizenship education. The explanation of an AHA-sponsored committee on "history inquiry" chaired by Edgar Dawson (secretary of the new National Council for the Social Studies) was that history in the schools had to conform to the test of "civic values" (Hertzberg 1981). From the inception of NCSS, however, there have been disagreements within the social studies and historical professions over how history could best serve its citizenship education function. In the face of changes in historiography, social welfare issues, and educational reforms, the underlying arguments about the aims of history education have nevertheless been amazingly constant.

The Aims of History Education

As noted above, NCSS has been marked by a continuing tension between history as a feature of cross-disciplinary citizenship education and history as a separate discipline "for its own sake." This distinction has been a specious argument, however, as advocates of history for its own sake also make citizenship claims for it. In 1925, Henry Johnson argued that disciplinary history was "the road that really reaches the desired end … what matters now" (Lybarger 1991, 7). In the 1950s, Arthur Bestor argued that disciplinary history was essential for citizens because it "promoted the perspectives on change which were essential to

a changing society" and was a "corrective to the contemporaneity of the social sciences" (Hertzberg 1981, 90).

In general, the argument has not been over citizenship or disciplinary history, but over the aims of history instruction. "History for its own sake" advocates have tended to view history education as a form of cultural transmission, whereas cross-disciplinary advocates more often have advocated a cultural transformation view. In addition, there is an "ownership" conflict between professional historians and those who translate history into curriculum. Bestor, for instance, did not simply argue for disciplinary history; he also railed against "the arrogance of those secondary-school educators who believe that they own the schools and can mold them as they please without regard to the rest of the scientific, intellectual and professional life of the nation" (1953, 11). In the 1960s and 1970s, critics again expressed concern that history education was in disarray, this time lost in a sea of social studies electives and special history courses often women's history and African American history—rather than in more traditional mainstream courses (e.g., Kirkendall 1975; Gross 1977; Kownslar 1976).

In its most recent incarnation, disciplinary study appears as part of a program of "cultural literacy." Lynn Cheney (1987), for instance, claimed that separate disciplinary history as a form of cultural transmission was necessary for cultural survival.

Other advocates of a separate discipline perspective have claimed that an integrated social studies field does not respect historical scholarship and dilutes both method and content. They hark back to a mythic golden age of education when students shared both a body of historical knowledge and a common historical vocabulary (e.g., Ravitch 1989; Evans 1989; Hertzberg 1981). Still others argue that social studies has failed in its citizenship role, leaving only "knowledge" as the purview of the field. James Leming (1992), for instance, suggests that social studies concentrate on "[t]he development of an *accurate knowledge of our American history, our traditions* and the social world" (310) (italics mine). As Seixas (1993) notes, cultural transmission approaches such as these essentially are conservative, tending to maintain the status quo. They also tend to hark back to a vision of objective, scientific history that ignores almost a century of historical and social arguments about what constitutes science, objectivity, and history.

Advocates of a cross-disciplinary or integrated social studies model also claim that history should contribute to civic education, but their aim has more often been cultural transformation rather than transmission. Aligned with the social welfare roots of social studies, they tend to point forward to a (perhaps mythic) golden age marked by citizens able to use history both to understand and evaluate current events and to participate in solving social and economic problems. In 1932, "A Charter for the Social Studies" explicitly argued for "ethical" social studies rather than indoctrination. Later, in *The Future of the Social Studies* (1939), James Michener called for a history curriculum with an emphasis on social and economic problems. By the 1940s and early 1950s, there were calls for more local history as a way of interesting youth in the betterment of their local communities. Adherents of this view argued for "history as culture change" (Krug 1970). Particularly in the period since the 1960s, advocates of history as cultural transformation have reconceptualized history to make it more "relevant" to a society experiencing major upheavals. Staughton C. Lynd (1970) described this as "guerrilla history," arguing that history should lead to social action, particularly on behalf of oppressed peoples. Historians could not afford to be the impartial observers of scientific history; historians were obligated to be social activists. A sense of history, according to Lynd, developed when an individual sensed that his or her actions were important and would influence the future of humanity.

From these two positions—history as cultural transmission and history as cultural transformation—flow several other differences in emphasis within NCSS and between NCSS and other groups. To begin with, cultural transmission advocates tend to emphasize the development of narrative history, i.e., the story well told. They argue that history is crucial to a people's sense of identity. Without some common history, a culture as diverse as the United States, for instance, is in danger of fragmentation (cf. Ravitch and Schlesinger 1990). Hence, the national story well told represents both an attempt at historical synthesis and an important way in which culture can be transmitted and preserved.

Cultural transformation, on the other hand, emphasizes analysis—sources well scrutinized—in which the historian or student develops a scholarly skepticism in regard to sources.[2] From this perspective no single narrative, not even the best told story, can possibly be our story as no one model of history can serve all institutions or all students (Robinson and Kirman 1986). Instead, different narratives speak to and against each other. And, as they do so, they interpret the past in light of the present (cf. White 1982). Part of teaching and learning history, then, would be to subject all historical narratives—well told or not—to scrutiny and skepticism.

Furthermore, advocates of cultural transmission tend to emphasize chronological history, while those advocating cultural transformation often suggest organization around themes. The "core curriculum" was one attempt at thematic organization. Some of the Project Social Studies materials of the 1960s represent other efforts. The differences between these perspectives can be seen most recently in the History Standards project. The standards currently are organized chronologically with a single periodization for U.S. history and another for world history (NCHS 1994). In an early critique of the U.S. standards, the NCSS Task Force on History Standards recommended an organization based on themes and questions rather than chronology. The Task Force argued that themes and questions were a more powerful organizing tool for history instruction, and were more likely to help students make connections between different aspects of history and their own lives. [3]

A final distinction between history for cultural transmission and history for cultural transformation occurs around the issue of teaching history. A cultural transmission model tends to describe history as something one learns (a chronological narrative or body of information) while a cultural transformation model tends to describe history as something one does (historical inquiry). On the one hand, the advocates of cultural transmission ask how students can be expected to conduct historical inquiries if they know little or no history. They also argue that U.S. students, at least, have provided ample evidence that they do not know much history (Ravitch and Finn 1988). On the other hand, cultural transformation advocates suggest that children do not retain much historical data because it has only been presented to them as information to be learned—a finished product—rather than as an ongoing interpretive activity that has relevance to their lives (Seixas 1993; Holt 1990b). In sum, the two positions define historical knowledge quite differently.

What Is Historical Knowledge?

If NCSS had embodied a coherent view of historical knowledge for its entire seventy-five-year history, it would have been completely out of step with the historiography of the same period. History in the twentieth century has been remarkable for its shifts and upheavals. A discipline that began the century searching for truth ends the century in the throes of post-modernist angst, questioning "truth" claims and wondering what constitutes historical knowledge. The dominant narrative of national history with which the century began fractures into multiple, and often contesting, narratives toward its close (Appleby, Hunt, and Jacob 1994; Kessler-Harris 1990; Seixas 1993). Ironically, but probably predictably, the century also ends with the breakup of the historical canon in which NCSS was invited to participate and the creation of a hotly contested new canon—the history "standards."

Against this backdrop, it is particularly challenging to think about what counts as historical knowledge. American historians, over the course of the last seventy-five years, have assumed four major historiographic stances that parallel the debates about history and historical knowledge in NCSS. In the 1920s and 1930s, progressive historians generally subscribed to some version of scientific history: assuming a position of impartiality, identifying "facts" by the rigorous examination of archival and original sources, and developing interpretations that organized and explained the facts. Historical knowledge was derived mainly from the political life of nations but with a progressive emphasis on the struggle between special interests and ordinary people. Historians' interest in social progress did introduce new categories of historical knowledge (the conditions of everyday life, including household living and work practices of women and children), but social history remained on the margins of the mainstream historical narrative until the 1960s.

Political history also remained the dominant feature of the secondary social studies curriculum, although it sometimes appeared in "core" curriculums under the rubric of "culture" or "civilization" (Hertzberg 1981; Michener 1939). In "unit" instruction at the elementary level, features of social history were more likely to appear. Young children re-created the daily living and work practices of earlier times, for example, in the study of wool from "sheep to shirt," and the reenactment of pioneer and Native American life. Unit instruction made the lives of at least some ordinary people a proper subject of investigation in the elementary classroom.

In the 1940s and 1950s, historians of the "consensus" school rejected the conflict model of the progressives. Instead, they focused on uncovering a broadly shared set of values that, they argued, overrode ethnic and class distinctions. Consensus historians were interested in intellectual history and often described the American intellectual landscape as stultifying rather than conflicted. Nonetheless, intellectual history functioned much as did social history; it elaborated on the mainstream political narrative. Political history also remained the backbone of school history, although some historians, led by Arthur Bestor, accused "educationists" and social studies advocates of ignoring historical knowledge in favor of courses in "life adjustment" and the like. In fact, the only change in what counted as historical knowledge in schools during this period appears to have been a move away from the study of individual European nations and toward world history (Downey 1985; Hertzberg 1981). Despite the fact that little had changed in the status of school history, a bitter conflict arose between some members of NCSS and some historians over a perceived decline in emphasis on history. Underlying the arguments over the amount of history in the schools, however, lay the old debate over the aims of history instruction and the type of history those aims required. The effects of this dispute, among both historians and social studies educators, have persisted. Echoes of the same charges and countercharges continue to be heard in current debates over the place of history in the social studies curriculum.

By the 1960s, social history moved from the margins to center stage of historical scholarship. This period is a fascinating time, both for the history profession and for NCSS. A conflation of factors—strands pulled forward from previous times, the social and political tensions of the 1960s, developments in other social sciences, and available funding—led to a period of intense activity. In a society torn by civil rights, women's rights, and antiwar protests, it was difficult to maintain the illusion that a unified history of progress and consensus was possible. In the face of resurgent populism, it was also hard to maintain that a study of political elites could adequately reflect broad national social and political processes. Instead, the new social historians assumed that society was divided by race, class, gender, and ethnicity, and that traditional historical sources were inadequate for their needs. They turned instead to the French Annales school. These historians concerned themselves with underlying structures that evolved over a long period of time—population shifts, trade patterns, and the like. They studied the lives and habits of ordinary people and searched for the frameworks that shaped the past. In so doing, they used quantitative methods to study local areas in depth. This effort was not unlike methods already in use in the behavioral sciences. In addition, quantitative studies gave the illusion of objectivity that seemed lacking in traditional descriptive history. Joining with their colleagues in the behavioral sciences, then, historians began a search for ordering principles, theories of systematic relations, and the structures of social institutions.

The turn to quantification and the search for structure paralleled developments in social studies education. The new social studies of the 1960s was founded on the search for the structure of the disciplines and the patterns of inquiry that supported the disciplines. In 1966, Edwin (Ted) Fenton, professor of history and co-director of the Social Studies Curriculum

Development Center at Carnegie Institute of Technology, explained how the "new history" and the "new social studies" were related. Fenton described the new history as "the development in the student of certain attitudes and values, the use of a mode of inquiry, and the attainment of knowledge about ... content" (Fenton 1966, 325). He went on to argue that learning "how to discover things for themselves" was crucial to students when "the new scholarly knowledge amassed in the last decade or so probably equals the total that mankind has discovered in the previous centuries of his existence" (326). This emphasis on the structure of history was not without its critics. Mark Krug (1967), for example, began his book *History and the Social Sciences* with a "premise and a hope that there are vast numbers of social studies professors and social studies teachers who have serious doubts about the 'new' social studies" (ix). While he was enthusiastic about students' doing historical inquiry, he was less sanguine about the emphasis on structure, concepts, and generalizations and worried that much that was distinctly historical would be lost in the "new" social studies.

The emphasis on inquiry learning and the structure of history as a discipline broadened the definition of historical knowledge to include the process of doing history. Given this perspective, the transmission of information without attention to process inaccurately represented historical thinking. Teachers were exhorted to help students learn history through the introduction of combinations of primary and secondary sources rather than textbooks, and through the use of such techniques as simulations rather than recitations (cf. Oliver and Shaver 1966).[4] In arguing for the reliance on doing history rather than reading about it, however, educators recognized that teachers also had to know more about both the content and processes of history. Fenton was particularly emphatic about the need for a solid foundation in history for

teachers. He suggested that college teaching would have to use the inductive teaching practices designed for the new social studies projects in order to adequately prepare teachers for the new history.

Despite the funds channeled into these history projects and the best hopes of their proponents, the projects had little direct impact on classroom instruction. The textbound cultural transmission model prevailed in most classrooms (Stanley 1985). In another sense, however, the structure of the disciplines movement and the new social history did have an impact on conceptions of historical knowledge. First, the new history shifted individuals and groups who had been on the margins of mainstream history toward the center. In fits and starts, amidst acrimony and resistance, a more inclusive history emerged. Along with articles and presentations at meetings, an NCSS Bulletin, *Teaching American History: New Directions* (Downey 1982), traced some of these developments in the history profession and provided teachers with both bibliographic help and teaching activities to support inclusion of the new history in the classroom. Second, the idea that history had a structure distinct from other disciplines—that history existed "in the world"—was called into question by the ways in which the new social history and the curriculum projects blurred disciplinary boundaries, borrowing method and content from other social sciences. Historians began to reconsider the foundation of their work, including the nature of their discipline, the possibility of objectivity, and the validity of truth claims.

In the last decade and a half, postmodernism has further challenged the way in which many scholars view historical knowledge (e.g., Appleby, Hunt, and Jacob 1994; Kessler-Harris 1990; Seixas 1993). From one post-modernist perspective, history does not exist as a discipline "in the world"; rather, it exists "in the head" as a cultural frame (Geertz

1983). Historical ideas are not objective facts so much as cultural artifacts that have meaning within particular discourse communities (e.g., Bakhtin 1986; Swales 1990; Todorov 1982). Thus, historical knowledge can never be fixed, nor described in terms of "truth." Instead, it is best understood as a constantly evolving creation of historians who operate within a cultural context. The "discipline" of history, then, is subject to an equally evolving set of rules that are tested in dialogue with others in communities of inquiry (Levstik and Pappas 1992). This means that the whole notion of "historical knowledge" becomes problematic. With no ground of truth to stand on, critics argue, only fragmentation and uncertainty can exist (Appleby, Hunt, and Jacob 1994; Kessler-Harris 1990).

This view seriously challenges common practice in schools. There, history is still generally conceived of as a body of knowledge objectively determined. On a number of levels, seeing history as objective is a much less threatening idea than seeing it as inherently subjective. How are teachers to negotiate through the land mines of historical subjectivity? How can they know what to teach amid the competing claims of different advocacy groups? Critics worry about how new conceptions of history will play out in classroom settings. They claim that history will be weakened by a "presentism" that serves neither present needs nor historical accuracy. These critics argue against a move away from the goal of objectivity and advocate a curriculum in which history is taught "for its own sake"— whatever that might be. And that, of course, is the problem. It is hard to argue, given the current state of historical discourse, that there is any such thing as "history for its own sake," much less that such a history would not serve some present purpose.

On the other hand, modern social history with its emphasis on multiple and often competing perspectives potentially provides exciting possibilities for social studies curriculum development. As Alice Kessler-Harris (1990) notes, "[F]undamental to social history is a respect for the cultures of different groups and a recognition of the power of diversity... [I]t attempts to understand how a society mediates the competing claims of order and authority, of freedom and rebellion" (178).

From a classroom perspective, this position means that the history of racial and ethnic groups, labor and class history, and gender history fundamentally alter the traditional curriculum. The traditional historical narrative cannot be reformed simply by adding a few women or people of color to the historical portrayal. Instead, "it requires repainting the earlier pictures, because some of what was previously on the canvas was inaccurate and more of it misleading" (Gordon 1990, 186). History instruction, then, might involve studying the creation of a "public culture": how people in other times measured their own lives, how groups and individuals exercise power publicly and privately, how society mediates competing claims between order and protest, and how political and social meanings are transmitted through language (Kessler-Harris 1990). This notion certainly means that the history curriculum is more complex, but not that it disintegrates. Instead, the focus of history instruction shifts from the development of a mainstream narrative to attention to the relationships among groups of people, illuminating their differing conceptions of social reality and the actions that grow out of those conceptions. This perspective provides substantial common ground with social studies educators whose aims are cultural transformation.

As yet, no new consensus appears to be growing out of these differing perspectives. If anything, the rhetoric has heated up in the last decade and a half. In a conservative era, history has been the focus of a neonationalist movement that harks back to the 1950s rather than to the historiography of the last thirty

years.[5] The predominant school reform proposals of the period have resurrected Arthur
Bestor's rhetoric and limited historical vision,
reemphasizing Eurocentric history in the face
of an increasingly diverse population, arguing
for separate disciplinary studies when the
boundaries of the disciplines have long since
been breached, and promoting history as
a story well told when the whole concept of
"story" has been fundamentally altered.

Negotiating the History Landscape

Clearly, NCSS has not been immune to the
changes that have buffeted the history profession or from the arguments about the aims of
history. Both cultural transmission and cultural transformation aims, for instance, have
coexisted in NCSS since its inception. Various
individuals hold both perspectives to some
degree. In 1982, James Banks, then President
of NCSS, wrote that "[e]ducators should strive
to attain a delicate balance between educating
students to be bearers of a continuous cultural
tradition and educating them to be social critics interested in social change" (Banks 1982,
x). More recently, James Barth (1994) defined
social studies as "the heritage of a nation," but
defined that heritage as one requiring citizens
who were active decision-makers. To some
extent, NCSS has striven to reflect just this
balance among often contending perspectives.

Plagued by claims that social studies fails to
respect disciplinary scholarship, NCSS has
tried to provide social studies educators with
regular updates on new scholarship. Beginning
in 1934, the organization published a series of
bulletins, yearbooks, and articles in which
social studies educators and historians commented on current trends and issues in the
field. Sometimes these articles were strictly
historical, i.e., updates on some aspect of history. Sometimes historians and educators
worked in tandem; historians provided an
update on the discipline, and educators pro-

vided suggestions for teaching (cf. Downey
1982; Hertzberg 1989). In 1982, a group of
historians and educators interested in promoting better history education organized the
Special Interest Group for History Teachers
(SIGHT) within NCSS. SIGHT continues to
sponsor history-related sessions at NCSS
Annual Meetings, publishes a newsletter for
members, and serves as an advocacy group
within NCSS.

NCSS has also been represented on
several history-related projects, including
the National Assessment of Educational
Progress U.S. History Assessment in 1988 and
1994, the History Standards project in 1994,
and the National Commission on Social
Studies in the Schools in 1989. In working
with some of these groups, NCSS has had to
weigh the desire to participate in the dialogue
over the place of history in the schools and
the impact of final reports that may not
represent the thinking of individuals in significant factions within NCSS. This problem
has been particularly difficult during the
almost simultaneous development of national
history standards and social studies standards.
While NCSS hopes that its social studies
standards will serve as an umbrella for standards developed for separate subject areas,
conflict remains between the separate disciplinary aims of some groups and individuals and
the cross-disciplinary and citizenship goals of
social studies.

In its debates over the place of history in
the schools, NCSS has generally supported
history advocacy groups and cooperated with
history organizations such as AHA and OAH
(Organization of American Historians). Interestingly, however, NCSS has devoted little
time and attention to one area in which it
might have been expected to develop expertise: development of a research base on teaching and learning history. In a 1990 review of
research, Downey and Levstik noted that the
"research base for teaching and learning histo-

ry is thin and uneven" (400). Brophy (1990), in his analysis of the state of elementary school social studies, came to similar conclusions. Although much speculation has occurred about the development of historical thinking (cf. Hoge and Crump 1988; Laville and Rosenzweig 1982; Egan 1979, 1982), only recently have researchers actually conducted studies of the development of historical thinking with K-12 students. These studies question prior assumptions regarding children's conceptions of historical time and causation (e.g., Barton and Levstik 1994; Downey 1994; Levstik and Barton 1994); historical significance (e.g., Seixas 1994a, 1994b); the effects of particular modes of instruction (e.g., Brophy, VanSledright, and Bredin 1992; Epstein 1994; Gabella 1994; Levstik 1993; Wineburg 1992); historical empathy and perspective taking (Portal 1990; Shemilt 1984); and teacher background (e.g., Evans 1988). Much of this research challenges the "expanding environments" scope and sequence for the elementary school curriculum as well as Piagetian notions of stage constraints on learning (Downey and Levstik 1990; Laville and Rosenzweig 1982). These studies also raise questions about the formulation of "historical thinking" as currently outlined in the proposed national history standards, and about the effectiveness of an emphasis on decontexualized bits of information.

Finally, NCSS has only recently begun to devote time and attention to the special needs of elementary school instruction. The history profession has also tended to concentrate on secondary curriculum. As a result, there are relatively few resources available to help educators think about what a history program might look like at this level. The expanding environments curriculum has long been the de facto national curriculum organization at the elementary level. Although this arrangement has come under increasing attack over the last decade, NCSS has not provided clear alterna-

tive curricula.[6] Part of the problem is the link between the expanding environments model and Piagetian developmental theory. Perhaps as new research demonstrates that young children *can* think historically in ways that run counter to Piagetian theories, a more substantive dialogue will develop over whether children *should* study history from the very beginning of their schooling (cf. Thornton 1990).

Conclusions

As I conclude this chapter, I see several possible futures for history education and NCSS. On the one hand, the domination of neoconservative reform measures could continue. History would serve to transmit a narrow band of mainstream culture, maladapted to the needs of a multicultural society. History teaching and assessment would be framed by a "story," supported by masses of information and unconnected to critical thinking, cultural transformation, or civic participation. Alternately, we could have business as usual— the most likely scenario based on the impact of previous reform efforts. History instruction will continue to be textbound, with minor attention to cultural diversity but little active involvement of students in the analysis of historical sources or the development of historical interpretations. Or, we could make common cause with the new social historians and work together toward an educational synthesis centered on the study of the creation of public culture. This view of history, it seems to me, is the one option most likely to meet the citizenship aims of social studies while fully exploiting the disciplinary contributions of history. By focusing on the relationships among groups of people, how they exercise power privately and publicly, and what they do when that power is threatened, we also focus on issues critical to our students' current needs.

It is not enough for us to simply accept historians' views of history. We must enter this endeavor as equal partners with important expertise. We must conduct the careful research necessary in order to understand both the development of historical thinking in young people and the classroom practices that support historical engagement. With a solid body of research, we can better develop the kind of instruction that makes history exciting and worthwhile for young learners and better consider how history contributes to the larger goals of social studies.

Notes

1 The definition adopted by NCSS in 1993, while declaring that social studies is "an integrated study," whose aim is "civic competence," is still non-specific enough to embrace a wide variety of interpretations and to generate continuing debate about how history and the social sciences further the goal of civic competence.

2 While it is not possible to adequately address this issue here, I recommend Novick's *That Noble Dream: The Objectivity Question* and the *American Historical Profession* (1988) and Appleby, Hunt, and Jacob's *Telling the Truth About History* (1994) both of which provide insightful, in-depth and, I think, reasonably balanced discussion of the origins of this difference.

3 In the rationale presented for the organizing themes and questions for K-12 Social Studies, *NCSS Task Force on History Standards* stakes out a position for history within a cross-disciplinary social studies framework, emphasizing the inquiry aspects of history instruction rather than assuming a single chronological narrative, as follows:

This plan has several strengths to recommend it. First, the use of questions under each theme emphasizes the inquiry aspects of social study, gives teachers some idea of the kinds of questions that might be pursued or adapted, and better represents the kinds of issues that historians and social scientists pursue. Second, these themes are more representative of the integrative nature of history and the social sciences. Third, these

themes are applicable to studies of the U. S. and the world, and may encourage students better to see the connections between their own country and the rest of the world.

4 By 1966, history projects were organized at Education Services, Inc., Amherst, Northwestern, the Newton (Mass.) Public Schools, the Cleveland Center, and Carnegie Institute of Technology. While several of these projects attempted to identify and teach the "structure of history," there was little consensus on what that structure might be. Fenton suggested that the structure of history meant the analytical questions historians put to data. He went on to describe how that process was conducted in "both history and the more rigorous social sciences" (Fenton 1966, 2).

5 One school system in Florida, for instance, recently mandated that children be taught that the United States is superior to all other countries in the world. While this may be an extreme case of neoconservative nationalism, it is indicative of the fervor of the movement.

6 The NCSS statement on Early Childhood and Elementary Social Studies does not really address this issue, and while the new NCSS journal, *Social Studies and the Young Learner*, has printed several articles on history for young learners, it hasn't really addressed the expanding horizons curriculum. Instead, that discussion has been largely confined to the NCSS research journal, *Theory and Research in Social Education*, where it is less likely to have an impact on practitioners.

References

Alleman, J., and J. Brophy. "Trade-Offs Embedded in the Literary Approach to Early Elementary Social Studies." *Social Studies and the Young Learner* 6, no. 3 (1994): 6-8.

Appleby, J., L. Hunt, and M. Jacob. *Telling the Truth about History.* New York: Norton, 1994.

Bakhtin, M. M. *Speech Genres and Other Late Essays.* Translated by V. W. McGee. Austin: University of Texas Press, 1986.

Banks, J. "Introduction." In *Teaching American*

History: New Direction, edited by M. Downey, ix-xi. NCSS Bulletin 67. Washington, D.C.: NCSS, 1982.

Barth, J. L. "Social Studies Is the Heritage of a Nation." In *The Future of the Social Studies*, edited by M. Nelson, 11-16. Boulder, Colo.: Social Science Education Consortium, 1994.

Barton, K. C. "History Is More Than Story: Expanding the Boundaries of Elementary Learning." Paper presented at the annual meeting of the National Council for the Social Studies, Nashville, Tenn., November 1993.

Barton, K. C., and L. S. Levstik. "Back When God Was Around and Everything: Elementary Children's Understanding of Historical Time." Paper presented at the annual meeting of the American Educational Research Association, New Orleans, La., April 1994.

Bestor, A. "Anti-Intellectualism in the Schools." *New Republic* 128 (1953): 11-13.

Bradley Commission on History in Schools. *Building a History Curriculum: Guidelines for Teaching History in Schools.* 1989.

Brinkley, A. "Prosperity, Depression, and War, 1920-1945." In *The New American History*, edited by E. Foner, 119-41. Philadelphia, Pa: Temple, 1990.

Brophy, J. "Teaching Social Studies for Understanding and Higher-Order Application." *The Elementary School Journal* 90, no. 4 (1990): 351-417.

Brophy, J., B. A. VanSledright, and N. Bredin. "Fifth Graders' Ideas about History Expressed Before and After Their Introduction to the Subject." *Theory and Research in Social Education* 20 (1992): 440–89.

Cheney, L. V. *American Memory: A Report on the Humanities in the Nation's Schools.* Washington, D.C.: National Endowment for the Humanities, 1987.

Downey, M. "After the Dinosaurs. Elementary Children's Chronological Thinking." Paper presented at the Annual Meeting of the American Educational Research Association, New Orleans, April 1994.

Downey, M. *History in the Schools.* Bulletin 74. Washington, D.C.: NCSS, 1985.

———, ed. *Teaching American History: New Directions.* NCSS Bulletin 67. Washington, D.C.: NCSS, 1982.

Downey, M., and L. S. Levstik. "Teaching and Learning History." In *Handbook of Research on Social Studies Teaching and Learning*, edited by J. Shaver, 400-10. Macmillan, 1990.

Egan, K. *Educational Development.* New York: Oxford University Press, 1979.

———. "Teaching History to Young Children." *Phi Delta Kappan* 63 (1982): 439-41.

Engle, S. "The Future of Social Studies Education and NCSS." *Social Education* 34, no. 7 (1970): 778-86.

Epstein, T. L. "Sometimes a Shining Moment: High School Students' Creations of the Arts in Historical Contexts." *Social Education* 58, no. 3 (1994): 136-41.

Evans, R. W. "Diane Ravitch and the Revival of History: A Critique." *The Social Studies* 80, no. 3 (1989): 85-88.

———. "Lessons from History: Teacher and Student Conceptions of the Meaning of History." *Theory and Research in Social Education* 16, no. 3 (1988): 203-25.

Fenton, E. "History in the New Social Studies." *Social Education* 30, no. 5 (1966): 325-28.

Gabella, M. S. "Beyond the Looking Glass: Bringing Students into the Conversation of Historical Inquiry." *Theory and Research in Social Education* 22, no. 3 (1994): 340-63.

Geertz, C. *Local Knowledge: Further Essays in Interpretive Anthropology.* New York: Basic Books, 1983.

Gordon, L. "U.S. Women's History." In *The New American History*, edited by E. Foner, 185-210. Philadelphia, Pa.: Temple, 1990.

Gross, R. "The Status of Social Studies in the Public Schools of the U.S.: Facts and Impressions of a National Survey." *Social Education* 41, no. 3 (1977): 194-200.

Hertzberg, H. W. *Social Science Reform:1880–1980.* Boulder, Colo.: Social Science Education Consortium, 1981.

————. "History and Progressivism: A Century of Reform Proposals." In *Historical Literacy: The Case for History in American Education*, edited by P. Gagnon. Boston: Houghton Mifflin, 1989.

Hirsch, E. D., *Cultural Literacy: What Every American Needs to Know.* Boston: Houghton Mifflin, 1987.

Hoge, J. D., and C. Crump. *Teaching History in the Elementary School.* Bloomington, Ind.: ERIC Clearinghouse for Social Studies/Social Science Education, 1988.

Holt, T. C. "African-American History." In *The New American History*, edited by E. Foner, 211-32. Philadelphia, Pa.: Temple, 1990. (1990a)

————. *Thinking Historically: Narrative, Imagination, and Understanding.* New York: College Entrance Examination Boards, 1990. (1990b)

Kessler-Harris, A. "Social History." In *The New American History*, edited by E. Foner, 163-84. Philadelphia, Pa.: Temple, 1990.

Kirkendall, R. "The Status of History in the Schools." *Journal of American History* 62, no. 2 (1975): 557.

Kownslar, A. "The Status of History: Some Views and Suggestions." *Social Education* 40, no. 6 (1976): 447-49.

Krug, M. *History and the Social Sciences.* Waltham, Mass.: Ginn, 1967.

————. "The Future of the Social Studies: Issues, Trends, and Opportunities." *Social Education* 34, no. 7 (1970): 768-76.

Laville, C., and L. W. Rosenzweig. "Teaching and Learning History: Developmental Dimensions." In *Developmental Perspectives on the Social Studies*, edited by L. W. Rosenzweig, 54-66. Bulletin 66. Washington, D.C.: NCSS, 1982.

Leinhardt, G., I. L. Beck, and C. Stainton, eds. *Teaching and Learning History.* Hillsdale, N.J.: Lawrence Erlbaum Associates, 1994.

Leming, James. "Ideological Perspectives within the Social Studies Profession: An Empirical Examination of the 'Two Cultures' Thesis." *Theory and Research in Social Education* 20, no. 3 (1992): 293-312.

Levstik, L. S. "Building a Sense of History in a First-Grade Classroom." In *Advances in Research on Teaching*, Vol. 4 (1993), edited by J. Brophy, 1-31. Greenwich, CT: JAI Press, 1994.

Levstik, L. S., and K. C. Barton. "They Still Use Some of Their Past: Historical Salience in Elementary Children's Chronological Thinking." Paper presented at the annual meeting of the American Educational Research Association, New Orleans, La., April 1994.

Levstik, L., and C. Pappas. "New Directions in Historical Understanding." *Theory and Research in Social Education* 20, no. 4 (1992): 369-85.

Lubove, R. *The Professional Altruist: The Emergence of Social Work as a Career.* Cambridge, MA: Harvard University Press, 1965.

Lybarger, M. B. "The Historiography of Social Studies: Retrospect, Circumspect, and Prospect." In *Handbook of Research on Social Studies Teaching and Learning*, edited by J. Shaver, 3-26. Macmillan, 1991.

Lynd, S. "Guerrilla History." *Social Education* 34, no. 5 (1970): 525-27.

Michener, J. A. "The Problem of the Social Studies." In *The Future of the Social Studies, Curriculum Series: Number One*, edited by J. A. Michener, 1-5. Washington, D.C.: NCSS, 1939.

National Center for History in the Schools. "National Standards for United States History, Pre-Publication Copy." Los Angeles, Calif.: UCLA/NEH Research Program, 1994.

————. "National Standards for World History, Pre-Publication Copy." Los Angeles, Calif.: UCLA/NEH Research Program, 1994.

National Commission on Social Studies in the Schools. *Charting a Course: Social Studies for the 21st Century.* Washington, D.C.: National Commission on Social Studies in the Schools, 1989.

Novick, P. *That Noble Dream: The "Objectivity Question" and the American Historical Profession.* Cambridge: Cambridge University Press, 1988.

Oliver, D.W., and J. P. Shaver. *Teaching Public Issues in the High School.* Boston: Houghton Mifflin, 1966.

Portal, C. "Empathy." *Teaching History* 58 (1990): 36-38.

Ravitch, D. "The Revival of History: A Response."

The Social Studies 80, no. 3 (1989): 89-91.

Ravitch, D., and C. E. Finn. *What Do Our 17-Year Olds Know? A Report on the First National Assessment of History and Literature.* New York: Harper and Row, 1987.

Ravitch, D., and A. Schlesinger. "Statement of the Committee of Scholars in Defense of History." *Perspectives* 28, no. 7 (1990): 15.

Ricoeur, R. *Hermeneutics and the Human Sciences.* Translated by J. B. Thompson. Cambridge: Cambridge University Press, 1984.

Robinson, P., and J. M. Kirman. "From Monopoly to Dominance." In *Social Studies and Social Sciences: A Fifty-Year Perspective,* edited by S. P. Wronski and D. H. Bragaw. Bulletin 78. Washington, D.C.: NCSS, 1986.

Saxe, D. W. "Theory for Social Studies Foundations." *Journal of Educational Research* 62, no. 3 (1992): 259-77.

Seixas, P. "Parallel Crises: History and the Social Studies Curriculum in the USA." *Journal of Curriculum Studies* 25, no. 3 (1993): 235-50.

_____. "Student's Understanding of Historical Significance." *Theory and Research in Social Education* 22, no. 3 (1994a): 281-304.

_____. "Margins and Sidebars: Problems in Students' Understandings of Significance in World History." Manuscript submitted for publication, 1994b.

Shemilt, D. "Beauty and the Philosopher: Empathy in History and Classroom." In *Learning History,* edited by A. K. Dickinson, P. J. Lee, and P. J. Robers, 39-84. London: Heinemann, 1984.

Snedden, D. "History Studies in Schools: For What Purposes?" *Teachers College Record* 25 (1924): 7-9.

Stanley, W. B. "Recent Research in the Foundations of Social Education: 1976-1983." In *Review of Research in Social Studies Education, 1976-1983,* edited by W. Stanley. Bulletin 75. Washington, D.C.: NCSS, 1985.

Swales, J. M. *Genre Analysis: English in Academic and Research Settings.* Cambridge: Cambridge University Press, 1990.

Thornton, S. J. "Should We Be Teaching More History?" *Theory and Research in Social Education* 18, no. 1 (1990): 53-60.

Todorov, T. *Theories of the Symbol.* Ithaca, N.Y.: Cornell University Press, 1982.

Tryon, R. *The Social Sciences as School Subjects.* New York: Charles Scribner's Sons, 1934.

Vansledright, B., and J. Brophy. "Storytelling, Imagination, and Fanciful Elaboration in Children's Historical Reconstructions." *American Educational Research Journal* 29 (1992): 837-59.

Whelan, M. "History and the Social Studies: A Response to the Critics." *Theory and Research in Social Education* 20, no. 1 (1992): 2-16.

White, H. "The Politics of Historical Interpretation: Discipline and De-Sublimation." *Critical Inquiry* 9 (1982): 113-37.

Wineburg, S. S. "Probing the Depths of Students' Historical Knowledge." *Perspectives* 30, no. 3 (1992): 459-76.

NCSS *and Citizenship Education*

James P. Shaver
Utah State University

turbid. *1. muddy or cloudy from having the sediment stirred up ... 3. confused; perplexed; muddled.* New World Dictionary (2nd College Edition), 1968.

THE TASK OF EXPLICATING WHAT I PERCEIVE TO BE A CONFUSED AND muddled historical relationship between the National Council for the Social Studies (NCSS) and citizenship education has been perplexing. My own involvement in this enterprise—having spent a considerable portion of my professional life trying to understand and influence that relationship—was probably more impediment than help. Whether NCSS's conceptual connection to citizenship education is clearer now than it was over thirty years ago, even with recent action to take up the civic competence mantle officially, is not certain. It is clear that the discussion of underlying issues has not advanced noticeably. I have had a strong, disconcerting feeling of déjà vu in recent years as I have attended NCSS meetings and read NCSS publications, and heard and seen the same quandaries and perplexities discussed anew as if they presented fresh dilemmas, with solutions that were typically restatements of prior positions.

Another perplexity in writing this chapter arose from the defined nature of this volume. It is not, I was told, to be an NCSS house history (a relief to a non-historian). On the other hand, although the chapters are to be interpretive, personal statements, they are to be more than a spinning of personal recollections. Those are difficult lines to tread, made more perilous for me by the inclusion in the volume of a separate chapter on "the nature of social studies," which I presume will address the uncertainties in the meaning of "social studies" over the years of

NCSS's existence.

I have been involved in efforts both to focus NCSS's attention and activities on citizenship education and to define "social studies." These are inextricably intertwined endeavors, in my opinion, because obscurity vis-à-vis the meaning of social studies has been an obstacle to NCSS's pursuit of its citizenship education goal. That is, social studies—the central substantive term in the title National Council for the Social Studies—must be defined clearly and directly in terms of citizenship to provide the context within which the organization can focus its energy on citizenship education. Lack of clarity and concurrence in the meaning of social studies (even whether it is plural, "the social studies are ...", or singular, "social studies is ... ") has been a major source of sediment in the historically turbid NCSS-citizenship education relationship.

The Emergence of "Social Studies" and NCSS

In a retrospective volume on NCSS, most authors are likely to revisit the birth of the Council in 1921, including the genesis of the term "social studies" as a precursor to that event. The term had been in use previously; Saxe, among others, has suggested that "social studies" was coined at the end of the nineteenth century by social scientists who wanted to introduce a social activist dimension to their scholarly endeavors (1992, 259, 277). However, it is widely agreed that social studies gained currency as a curricular label through the 1916 Report of the Committee on Social Studies of the National Education Association (NEA) Commission on the Reorganization of Secondary Education (Hertzberg 1981; Lybarger 1991; Jenness 1990).

The 1916 report, if not the cause of the muddled NCSS-citizenship education relationship, certainly heralded that future. In that report, the social studies were (note the plural) defined as "those [studies] whose subject mat-ter relates directly to the organization and development of human society and to man [sic] as a member of social groups." The purpose of all schooling, according to the report, is "social efficiency," and the "conscious and constant purpose" of the social studies was to be the "cultivation of good citizenship" (quoted in Hertzberg 1981, 26). The curriculum proposed for grades 7-12 to accomplish that goal featured geography, European and American history, civics, and problems of democracy. (Although the academic disciplines included in the social studies were economics, geography, history, political science, and sociology, only history and geography were specified as subjects to be taught to students.) The question of whether social studies was to be an integrated curriculum focused on citizenship or to be a loosely connected group of subjects, some of which have direct and others inferred relationships to citizenship, was not addressed directly. The latter intent seems more likely.

The same vagueness in regard to the relationship between social sciences and history as curricular sources and citizenship as the major curricular goal was continued in NCSS's origin. NCSS was founded under the auspices of the American Historical Association (AHA). It shared annual meetings with the AHA for a number of years. (AHA also bestowed on NCSS the AHA teaching journal, *The Historical Outlook*, whose editor was the first NCSS President, and which preceded *Social Education* as the principal journal for NCSS members). Having been founded by historians and social scientists interested in secondary school instruction, NCSS from its start was imbued with a lack of clarity regarding the centrality of citizenship education to social studies. NCSS was to foster the association and cooperation of "teachers of education and others" to maximize "education for citizenship through social studies" (quoted in Lybarger 1991, 6). Yet, the charter of the organization defined the social studies as "history, economics, sociology, civics, geography and all modifications of subjects whose content as well as aim is social" (Barr, Barth, and Shermis 1977). The connection between goal and definition was not spelled out, laying the groundwork for a long-lasting turbidity in NCSS's relationship to citizenship education.

The Perpetual Paradox

As Hertzberg noted, two problems have plagued NCSS since its beginning (1981, 26). One is a definition that suggested that the social studies are a group of subjects (all, except for the incongruous civics and problems of democracy courses, being university disciplines) with implicit relationships to the organization's citizenship education goal—rather than a definition of social studies as a curricular area focused on citizenship education. The other problem is an unresolved ambivalence toward academic "learned societies" and professors. From the founding, domination by university scholars was viewed as undesirable, yet their involvement was seen as critical.

The two problems are not independent. With the NCSS founders largely coming from history and the social sciences, it is not surprising that the definition of the social studies embraced the various academic disciplines, with the assumption that study of those subjects would ipso facto effect good citizenship. "Scholacentrism" has pervaded NCSS, although not without criticism, since its inception, and has been a major element in the turbidity of the NCSS-citizenship education relationship.

The point is not that the study of history and the social sciences can make no contribution to effective citizenship. That it can is obvious. It is rather that, from its beginning, NCSS as an organization has not been clear about whether the study of history and the

social sciences as academic disciplines per se is sufficient for citizenship education, or whether a K-12 curriculum structured around citizenship is needed.

The issue spills over into assumptions about learning as well. Should instruction be based on the integrity of the disciplines, with a model of the well-read person in mind, as with a college or university course? Or should history and the social sciences be taught in the context of understanding the role and challenges of citizenship in a democratic society? Those questions oversimplify the complex matter of the relevance of the academic disciplines to competent citizenship and how students can be motivated to learn so that their schooling will influence their thinking and behavior as adult citizens. It does, however, embody an underlying lack of clarity that has confounded NCSS's endeavors since inception.

Contrasting Definitions

The issue can be sharpened by considering two contrasting definitions (see, e.g., Shaver 1967). One, commonly attributed to Edgar Wesley, originated with the Commission on the Social Studies. In this definition, the social studies are the social sciences simplified for pedagogical purposes. The other definition is that social studies is general education aimed at the preparation of citizens for participation in a democratic society. With the latter definition, social science and history content would be selected, organized, and taught based on the needs of democratic citizenship, rather than being based on the scholarly conceptual frames of social scientists and historians. The first definition does not necessarily preclude explicit, as well as implicit, instruction for citizenship aims. It simply places the emphasis instead on how to convey the content of academic disciplines. Nor does the second definition preclude history and social science units or courses. It simply asks, if they are to be part of the general curriculum, that there be a citizenship justification.

Wesley's definition has been predominant in K-12 social studies education and NCSS, contributing additional sediment to a turbid NCSS-citizenship education relationship. In fact, courses labeled "social studies" are rarely taught in public schools. Indeed, even though colleges of education have social studies curriculum and methods courses, most "social studies" teachers identify themselves as teachers, for example, of U.S. history, world civilization, or sociology. Moreover, few high school graduates can identify their junior and senior high school "social studies" courses, if asked to do so. As Shirley Engle noted in his NCSS presidential address in 1970, "Except as a noble purpose recognized and proclaimed by numerous committees and commissions on the social studies over the years, the Social Studies do not, in fact, exist today" (Engle 1971, 287).

The NCSS Conundrum

At its May 1975 meeting in Washington, D.C., the NCSS Board of Directors considered and approved several action items introduced by President Jean Tilford Claugus and then presented as motions by board members. One item, for which I moved approval as reported in the minutes of the meeting, was that "the NCSS Executive Director be encouraged to … continue efforts to define social studies education in terms of a central citizenship education thrust and to represent this orientation in his [NCSS] role." The wording was cautious. The Executive Director was "encouraged" (not "directed") to "continue efforts to define" (not to "act on the definition") "in terms of a central citizenship education thrust" (not "as the goal").

There was considerable opposition to a forthright statement of a citizenship-education-based definition, and Claugus's presentation of the item for discussion was, if not courageous, certainly controversial. It was not accidental that she made the suggestion the year before I was to be NCSS President. Our intent was to lay the foundation (abortively, as it turned out) for change during my term, but, ironically, she and I thought that opposition might be crystallized if a citizenship education advocate such as myself introduced the idea initially.

The debate over the definition of social studies had erupted occasionally among board members in the months before the May meeting. Given the organization's origin and continued ambiguous stance vis-à-vis the academic disciplines, it was not surprising that those against strong affirmation of citizenship education argued that asserting citizenship education as the central aim of social studies would alienate and drive from NCSS those university professors and others with disciplinary roots. Those advocating a strong citizenship education stance argued that a clear sense of purpose would have increased the integrity of NCSS. Even if that focus excluded some persons, or shaped their participation, the overall result would be an increase in membership. It was not suggested that those with history and social science orientations should be ostracized, but rather that their NCSS activities (e.g., presentations at annual meetings) should be focused on the contributions of the academic disciplines to citizenship education, not simply on how to teach the disciplines better. The perennial "the social studies as simplified social sciences versus social studies as citizenship education" paradox was at the center of the debate, with differing assumptions regarding the effects on membership.

The same issue had been posed clearly in 1970 by Shirley Engle, while President of NCSS, in an article, "The Future of Social Studies Education and NCSS," in the 50th anniversary issue of *Social Education* (Engle 1970). Engle challenged the definition of social studies as simplified social sciences and argued that it was time for NCSS "in its role as the responsible vane of social education to make some hard choices." The organization could, he noted,

> continue ... to constitute [itself] as a loose association ... held uneasily together by a common concern for the social education of children and youth ... [and] continue to avoid definition of our field of competence, confusing social education with the social sciences ... , [continuing] to afford our members a kind of smorgasbord of educational goodies and services, throughout which no cogent philosophic or pedagogical position runs, and from which, each according to his own interest or bent, one may choose to eat whatever he will ... [with] no clear and consistent position on social education and, for that matter, no clear definition of our field.

The alternative, he argued, was for NCSS to "define its field and focus its endeavor on the proper social education of citizens." Some social scientists who lack interest in social education might be excluded, he noted, but other persons would join who had not before because the previous organizational perspective had been both "too ambiguous and narrow" (Engle 1970, 780-81). In his presidential address later in the year, Engle again lamented the failure of NCSS members to grasp the distinction between the social sciences and social studies and the implications for citizenship education.

In my own NCSS presidential address in 1976, I returned to Shirley Engle's contention. Having been asked by the program planning committee for the annual meeting in Washington, D.C., to take a critical look at the "profession," my major theme was mindlessness in the field—i.e., lack of thought

about "purpose, and about the ways in which techniques, content, and organization fulfill or alter purpose" (Silberman 1970, 579). I not only questioned the continued assumption that social science and history courses automatically sum up to good citizenship education but challenged the notion that to focus NCSS on citizenship education would be too narrow or restrictive an approach. I proposed that all who joined NCSS should be asked

> to address the very significant question of what citizenship education should be in this society. The central query for NCSS should not be how to teach history, or economics, or political science better, but rather: what contribution does each have to make to citizenship education?

I also noted that, ironically, the answers to the question would likely also be responsive to queries about how to teach history and the social sciences better, because they would provide a Deweyan connection between content and problems that are real to students, rather than to academicians (Shaver 1977a). The failure to explicate and examine assumptions has led to the continuing paradox of an organization whose goal is citizenship education but which has been unable to step back and examine critically the influence of its history-social science roots on the pursuit of that goal.

NCSS and Citizenship Education

All of this is not to say that NCSS has ignored citizenship education. Various publications, including one I edited (Shaver 1977b), have addressed the topic, and citizenship education is often stated as a goal of the organization. The 1979 "Revision of the NCSS Social Studies Curriculum Guidelines" stated specifically: "The basic goal of social studies education is to prepare young people to be humane, rational, participating citizens"

(1979, 262). And the 1984 preliminary position statement of the NCSS Board of Directors on scope and sequence, prepared by a regional task force (to save travel funds), began, somewhat obtusely, with the acknowledgement that "social studies … derives its goals from the nature of citizenship in a democratic society"(1984, 251).

Then, paradoxically, we have the 1989 report of the Task Force on Curriculum of the National Commission on Social Studies in the Schools, published by NCSS, which co-founded the Commission with the American Historical Association. The task force's "working definition" was that social studies included history, geography, government and civics, economics, anthropology, sociology, and psychology, as well as subject matter drawn from the humanities, combined and used to develop a "systematic and interrelated study of people in societies, past and present" (*Charting a Course* 1989). Aside from the token mention of the humanities, largely ignored in the report, the definition is solidly social science-based with no mention of citizenship. Nevertheless, according to the report, a characteristic of the social studies curriculum is that it must "instill a clear understanding of the roles of citizens in a democracy and provide opportunities for active, engaged participation in civic, cultural and volunteer activities designed to enhance the quality of life in the community and in the nation (*Charting a Course*, 3).

This strangely inconsistent document, produced largely by persons from academic disciplines, aroused great ire and heated discussion, at least from some NCSS university members, during the NCSS annual meeting in St. Louis in 1989. On the one hand, the report seems an amazing piece of work to have come from an NCSS-sponsored task force; on the other hand, it seems an apt representation of the historically turbid NCSS-citizenship education relationship.

Thinking back to the need felt by the NCSS Board of Directors in 1975 to instruct the executive director, Brian Larkin, an economist, to represent the organization from a citizenship education perspective, I could not help but wonder in 1989 about the impact of the frame of reference of NCSS's executive director on the commission's makeup and, consequently, orientation. Fran Haley's background prior to assuming her NCSS position was with the Social Science Education Consortium. Among other executive directors, Paul Purta was a Catholic educator. Fine persons, but what organizational purpose or thrust did they signify?

The same could be said of Daniel Roselle, the likable, earnest, and sincerely erudite long-time editor of the official NCSS journal, *Social Education*. Roselle was strongly committed to the intrinsic value of the study of history and to a history-social science, especially history, base for the social studies.

It would hardly have been possible to infer from the potpourri of *Social Education* articles over the decades of Roselle's editorship or from other NCSS publications and the sessions at annual meetings (Shirley Engle's smorgasbord) anything except that the organization was committed to teaching history and the social sciences, with a smattering of concern for the possible inadequacies of that approach for citizenship education. A historical analysis of staff orientations as a factor in the turbid NCSS-citizenship education relationship could be instructive as NCSS officers look to the organization's next seventy-five years.

A New Definition

The 1975 NCSS Board of Directors' action directing the executive director "to continue efforts to define social studies in terms of a central citizenship education thrust" was not only obtuse but bordered on being covert. Aside from mention in my presidential address (actually, I unintentionally overstated the motion, as I said that the executive director was "instructed … that citizenship education is the focus of social studies education"), no public announcement was made. There was a reticence in the Board of Directors about advertising such a stance.

Not so eighteen years later. In the March/April 1992 issue of *The Social Studies Professional*, the NCSS newsletter, President Margit McGuire announced that the Board of Directors had begun action to establish a definition of social studies centered on civic competence. A definition was proffered for discussion and reaction:

> *Social studies is the integration of history, the social sciences, and the humanities to promote civic competence.*

In the January/February 1993 issue of *The Social Studies Professional*, President Charlotte Anderson announced with pride and excitement that NCSS, following a year of discussion, had officially accepted a "consensus definition of social studies," embracing "the promotion of civic competence as the central purpose of social studies." The definition, to be used as the basis for developing "social studies standards and for all [NCSS] documents and position statements," had changed slightly since 1992:

> *Social studies is the integrated study of the social sciences and humanities to promote civic competence.*

The definition statement went on to elaborate that "social studies provides coordinated, systematic study drawing upon" a variety of disciplines—the social sciences, history, philosophy, law, religion, and archaeology, and as appropriate, the humanities, mathematics, and science. The primary purpose is

> *To help young people develop the ability*

> *to make informed and reasoned decisions for the public good as citizens of a culturally diverse, democratic society in an interdependent world.*

Finally, there existed a clear, forthright statement of NCSS's intent in regard to citizenship education, even if the somewhat more circumscribed term "civic competence" was used. Although there was perplexity on the part of some, including me, about aspects of the definition—for example, the inclusion of religion as a discipline and the failure to mention behavior, such as effective action to influence policy and its implementation, as a crucial element of civic competence—the intent to focus NCSS seemed clear.

Implications

In itself, the new definition does not clear up the NCSS-citizenship education turbidity, but it does provide a context for discussion and action. For example, given the clear statement of purpose, a problem that Hazel Hertzberg (1981, 37) observed has plagued NCSS from its beginning might be addressed directly: that is, lack of clarity as to whether social studies is to be a "federation" or a "fusion" of subjects (or some combination thereof). What are the curricular implications of references in the definition to "integrated" and "coordinated, systematic study"? Will NCSS take a dramatic departure from the simplified-social-sciences approach to social studies or will it continue its smorgasbord approach in its publications and activities? (It may be noteworthy that although "social studies" is used in the singular in the 1993 definition, a social studies standards announcement cited by Charlotte Anderson in the May/June 1993 *The Social Studies Professional* refers to "the social studies." That reversion to the plural suggests a lack of conceptual consistency in the organization, with a strong residual of social science/history commitments.)

Despite the use of the plural in its title, however, NCSS's *Expectations of Excellence: Curriculum Standards for the Social Studies* does address "social studies," not "the social studies." The standards suggest implicitly that the real issue is not federation versus fusion (or some combination thereof), but a fundamental assumption about the role of the academic disciplines (especially the social sciences and history) in citizenship education. Is good citizenship a natural by-product of studying the academic disciplines, so that social science and history qua social science and history are sufficient? Or must there be attention to structuring social studies curricula that draw on the academic disciplines, but are not dictated by them? The curriculum standards clearly reflect the latter position.

What Impact?

It is ironic that, at what might be considered the height of professional identity for NCSS (with a definition and curriculum standards focused on civic competence/citizenship education), the new executive director, Martharose Laffey, raised basic questions about NCSS's identity and relevance in addressing the 1993 NCSS House of Delegates. She noted that despite the new definition, there is not yet "a unified professional identity.... We have a definition and yet we seem to be fragmented still as a profession." After deploring the greater recognition being accorded to the curriculum standards in history, civics, and geography, Laffey emphasized the need to "demonstrate more powerfully ... the importance of social studies ... [and] make a much stronger case for the relevance of social studies" (*Social Education* 1994, 202). Her pleas faintly echoed Shirley Engle's admonition in 1971 that "except as a noble purpose recognized and proclaimed by numerous committees and commissions ... ,

the social studies do not, in fact, exist today."

The role of NCSS in the current national curriculum standards effort is verification that Engle's observation applies today. There was something sad, almost pathetic, about the letter from Charlotte Anderson, as NCSS President, to President Clinton (printed in the May/June 1993 issue of *The Social Studies Professional*) decrying the absence of social studies in America 2000 and the Goals 2000: Educate America Act and pleading for his recognition of NCSS's standards and citizenship education efforts. Here, then, is the true conundrum and the ultimate turbidity in the NCSS-citizenship education relationship. Even with a clear definition of purpose, the organization lacks the clout to be a major player in the educational arena.

As a social studies advocate, NCSS lacks a "natural" interest group akin to those for science and mathematics, and for history and geography, which form around disciplinary identities. It also lacks the advocacy history that civics has in the Center for Civic Education. Moreover, NCSS lacks a base in public education. As noted above, there are few social studies curricula that are more than compendia of simplified history and social science courses; few, if any, textbooks titled "social studies"; few teachers who call themselves "social studies teachers," rather than identifying with a content area (e.g., U.S. history); few high school graduates who can tell you, despite (or because of) their K-12 experiences, what social studies is or are.

According to Martharose Laffey, NCSS in 1993 had about 22,000 members ("National Council for the Social Studies" 1994, 201). Of these, about 18,000 were individual members (the others were institutional subscribers), with, I estimate, perhaps 16,000 of them classroom teachers. This is a pitifully small proportion of the thousands who teach "social studies" in this country. Not only does NCSS lack a political base in public education, its potential to influence classroom instruction through organizational initiatives is very limited.

The future of social studies is most likely to be like the past that O. L. Davis, Jr., Suzanne Helburn, and I reported in 1979 as an NCSS task force to interpret studies of educational status sponsored by the National Science Foundation (Shaver, Davis, and Helburn 1980). Most "social studies" teachers will go on primarily as they have, teaching from their history-and-social-science-simplified text-books, largely not even aware of the NCSS intellectual tempest in a teapot. That is not to say that there will be no excellent, exciting teaching, but that most of it will continue to be subject oriented and textbook based, with only incidental, rather than intentional, direct citizenship/civic competence connections.

After a history of a muddled and confused relationship with citizenship education, NCSS has made a major step toward clarity of purpose that could provide structure for its activities, perhaps even including a lively debate over the essentials of civic competence curricula. The vestiges of "scholacentrism" and "academiphilia" that remain are sediment that will not, however, settle quickly or easily. And another fundamental element of perplexity remains. It is the organization's lack of conceptual or practical connection with the vast majority of elementary and secondary school classrooms in which a citizenship/civic competence agenda must be implemented and institutionalized if social studies is to be more than an organizational illusion.

References

In this discussion of citizenship and the beginnings of social studies and NCSS, I have relied heavily on three sources: Hertzberg (1981); Lybarger (1991); and Jenness (1990).

Barr, R. D., J. L. Barth, and S. S. Shermis. *Defining the Social Studies*. Bulletin 51. Washington, D.C.: National Council for the Social Studies, 1977.

Charting a Course: Social Studies in the 21st Century. Washington, D.C.: National Council for the Social Studies, 1989.

Engle, S. "The Future of Social Studies Education and NCSS." *Social Education* 34 (1970): 778–81, 795.

———. "Exploring the Meaning of the Social Studies." *Social Education* 35 (1971): 280-88, 344.

Hertzberg, H. W. *Social Studies Reform 1880-1980*. Boulder, Colo.: Social Science Education Consortium, 1981.

Jenness, D. *Making Sense of Social Studies*. New York: Macmillan, 1990.

Lybarger, M. B. "The Historiography of Social Studies: Retrospect, Circumspect, and Prospect." In *The Handbook of Research on Social Studies Teaching and Learning*, edited by James P. Shaver. New York: Macmillan, 1991.

"National Council for the Social Studies 37th House of Delegates Assembly, November 20-21, 1993, Nashville, Tennessee." *Social Education* 58 (April/May 1994): 199-205.

NCSS Board of Directors. "In Search of a Scope and Sequence in Social Studies." *Social Education* 48 (1984): 251.

"Revision of the NCSS Social Studies Curriculum Guidelines." *Social Education* 43 (1979): 262.

Saxe, D. W. "Framing a Theory for Social Studies Education." *Review of Educational Research* 62 (1992): 259, 277.

Shaver, J. P. "Social Studies: The Need for Redefinition." *Social Education* 31 (1967): 588-93.

———. "A Critical View of the Social Studies Profession." *Social Education* 41 (1977a): 300-307.

———. *Building Rationales for Citizenship Education*. Bulletin 52. Washington, D.C.: National Council for the Social Studies, 1977b.

Shaver, J. P., O. L. Davis, and S. W. Helburn. "The Status of Social Studies Education: Impressions from Three NSF Studies." *Social Education* 44 (1980): 150-53.

Silberman, C. E. *Crisis in the Classroom*. New York: Random House, 1970.

NCSS *and International/Global Education*

Jan L. Tucker
Florida International University

THIS CHAPTER EXAMINES PARTICI-
PATION BY THE NATIONAL COUNCIL
for the Social Studies (NCSS) in international
activities, beginning with the emergence of the
concept of the world as a global village in
the 1960s and using specific years, events, and
individuals as an organizing framework.

Leften S. Stavrianos, in his book *Lifelines from
the Past*, wrote that global perspectives are autobi-
ographical (1989). He is correct. Consider, for
example, James A. Michener, well-known author
and NCSS activist in the late 1930s. World War
II changed his profession: from social studies
teacher to navy officer and then to author.
How he wrote! But he has remained a reflective
and critically minded social studies teacher at
heart. His first book, *Tales of the South Pacific*, was
awarded the Pulitzer Prize in 1947; it was both
global and multicultural. Ahead of his time,
Michener showed us the way to the global
village, and we are proud of his social studies
beginnings.

1960s: The Global Village Arrives

We started thinking differently about ourselves as a nation in the 1960s. Paralleling the
significance of the civil rights movement and
the agony of the war in Southeast Asia was the
evolution of a new worldview. An intellectual
revolution took root.

Marshall McLuhan (1964) described the
global village with its people linked through
communications technology. Barbara Ward and
René Dubos (1972) and R. Buckminster Fuller
(1970) independently conceived the metaphor of
spaceship earth and described it as a closed life-
support system with its inhabitants accelerating
through time and space dependent upon each

other for survival. Rachel Carson (1962) astonished the public with her descriptions of the harmful consequences of the use of pesticides. Pierre Teilhard de Chardin (1964) wrote of the convergence of human aspirations and history into the noösphere, a progressive unification of humankind and intensification of our collective consciousness. Paul Ehrlich (1968) called our attention to the stunning exponential growth rate of world population and impending ecological catastrophe. Alvin Toffler (1970) warned of impending future shock. Barbara Ward and René Dubos (1972) coined the now-familiar notion of "thinking globally, acting locally." The Club of Rome ignited a global controversy regarding the rapid depletion of our non-renewable resources (Meadows et al. 1972). And biologist Lewis Thomas (1974) portrayed Earth as a single living cell.

Trends and events on a global scale played an important role in raising our consciousness. Those years were ending when the United States, with 5 percent of the world's population, both produced and consumed 40 percent of the world's resources and services. People around the world witnessed on broadcast television the assassination of President John F. Kennedy and the subsequent murder of his accused killer, Lee Harvey Oswald—events that still deeply trouble the nation. Offshore drilling failures washed vast quantities of crude oil onto Santa Barbara's unspoiled beaches and initiated a public outcry. American astronauts and Soviet cosmonauts reported on the radiant beauty of earth as seen from space. Who can forget Earthrise, the photo of multihued Earth ascending over the horizon of the moon's black and white landscape?

The global village had arrived, and the concept of global education for the schools began to take shape. It was a heady and exciting time to be a social studies teacher.

1964: The Glens Falls Story

In 1964, NCSS published the results of its three-year research and development program called *Improving the Teaching of World Affairs: The Glens Falls Story* (Long and King 1964). It covered all subjects and grade levels in the schools of Glens Falls, a city of 18,580 located in upstate New York. This major NCSS project offered social studies educators a new way to think about the world and schooling.

In many ways, the Glens Falls story reflected the standard nation-to-nation, foreign policy motif that characterized international education in the post-World War II era—with courses taught generally only in the high school social studies department. A closer examination of the program, however, reveals a more varied and a richer curriculum including, for example, the comparative study of student art from schools in several countries; merchandising and office practices in other countries; foods and families of the world; health and disease problems; mathematics as a means of international communication; and the technology of business and industry in other nations. This district wide, interdisciplinary, project-based approach was more than business as usual.

When Glens Falls developed a K-12 integrated curriculum reflecting the global village, it was ahead of its time. Glens Falls symbolized the decline of a strictly nation-centered, foreign relations, and textbook approach to international curricula in the schools. And it marked the beginning of a more global, interdisciplinary, and grassroots model.

Glens Falls is a grand account of NCSS leadership working in collaboration with a grassroots cadre of teachers, administrators, and community leaders. Local schools in the 1990s seeking a model for site-based school improvement can benefit from an examination of the Glens Falls story.

Glens Falls, however, made little impact on the social studies profession in the 1960s, largely because it had to compete for attention with the "new social studies." Well-financed and high-powered, the "new" social studies programs filled the national professional literature during the 1960s. As a budding but puzzled professional at the time, I can remember more than a few academic smirks about Glens Falls. NCSS had a "bottom up" program in global education, when "top down" subject matter was in vogue.

In retrospect, Glens Falls represents an especially heartening example of visionary grassroots NCSS leadership. Through its support of the Glens Falls program, NCSS was there at the beginning of the global village in social studies education.

I entered the world of NCSS and the global village in 1964. Already a seven-year veteran of the social studies classroom, I participated in my first NCSS annual meeting, held that year in St. Louis. I had developed and was teaching a sequential two-year course called Global Studies for ninth and tenth graders enrolled in the Indiana University Laboratory School located on the Bloomington campus. The basic textbook for the course was the first edition of *A Global History of Man*, by L. S. Stavrianos. It was supplemented by the "new social studies" experimental materials developed by the Anthropology Curriculum Study Project, under the guidance of Malcolm Collier and Robert G. Hanvey at the University of Chicago. At the St. Louis meeting, I made a presentation on "Teaching a Method of Inquiry," based on the Global Studies course. Adeline Brengle—an internationally minded local teacher in Bloomington and Elkhart, Indiana, and President of NCSS in 1966—influenced my thinking about leadership possibilities.

1968: The Birth of Global Education

In 1968, the idea of global education emerged from a landmark report by the Foreign Policy Association, funded by the U.S. Office of Education, titled *An Examination of Objectives and Priorities in International Education in U.S. Secondary and Elementary Schools*. In testimony to the importance of NCSS and its membership, Lee F. Anderson and James M. Becker, the report's authors, selected *Social Education* as the vehicle for introducing their findings and recommendations to the profession.

A veritable "who's who" of international educators and social scientists contributed to the November 1968 issue of *Social Education*, titled "International Education for the Twenty-First Century": Chadwick F. Alger, Anderson, Becker, Kenneth E. Boulding, Robert A. Harper, Bob G. Henderson, Herbert C. Kelman, Edith W. King, Charles A. McClelland, Roger G. Mastrude, Howard D. Mehlinger, Jerry R. Moore, Donald N. Morris, and Robert C. North. William A. Nesbitt, editorial director of the school services of the Foreign Policy Association, served as the guest editor of this special issue.

The authors argued that revolutionary changes on a global scale had outpaced a static curriculum and that the concept of "international" was losing its accuracy and utility. "The change from a collection of many lands and people to a system of many lands and peoples," according to Anderson, "was a profound change in the human condition." It became clear that a new term was needed to describe the changes. Global education was born.

As the idea of global education emerged during the 1960s, NCSS contributed to its development through such publications as, for example, the 1968 yearbook titled *International Dimensions in the Social Studies* (Becker and Mehlinger 1968). Although the title of the volume used the term "international," much of the content was "global"—a conceptual and semantic confusion that continues today.

The year 1968 was a precarious time for the introduction of global education and serves today as a powerful reminder of the influence of contemporary domestic events on educational change. During the Northern California Curriculum Conference held in September at Sausalito, I—as a rookie member of the Stanford University School of Education faculty—listened attentively as Becker and Anderson introduced the report of the Foreign Policy Association to social studies leaders in the San Francisco Bay Area. It was an exhilarating experience to hear this advocacy for global education proposed to California's most experienced social studies professionals, and I had expected a warm reception for the idea.

However, my most vivid memory of the conference is the skeptical response to the report by the participants. Preoccupied with the stunning events of life around them in 1968, the Sausalito conference participants were in no mood to hear about global interdependence. After all, across the Bay, college students were soon to face the bayonets of the National Guard—even though those very local events were the direct consequence of our involvement in Southeast Asia and therefore a perfect example of the importance of global studies. The negative reaction of the veteran Bay Area social studies educators to the idea of global education was a forecast of things to come throughout the nation at large.

The dynamic, turbulent nature of our national culture continues to impede the shift to a global view, despite the fact that the difference between foreign and domestic has practically disappeared. Social studies teachers confront this contradiction each day in their classrooms.

1970s: NCSS Joins the Global Village

Through its publications, NCSS played an important role during the 1960s in helping its members get in touch with the global village. The effort, however, was sporadic and largely reactive to people and forces outside NCSS. This changed during the 1970s when the NCSS Board of Directors became proactive, spurred on by activist NCSS Presidents, who included Howard D. Mehlinger, Anna S. Ochoa, and Stanley P. Wronski, with the support of the executive director, Brian J. Larkin.

Other NCSS members who made significant contributions to the development and execution of international policy and programs during this period included Sybil Abbott (Reno), James L. Barth (West Lafayette), John Chapman (Lansing), Wentworth Clark (Orlando), H. Thomas Collins (Washington, D.C.), John J. Cogan (Minneapolis), Billie A. Day (Washington, D.C.), M. Eugene Gilliom (Columbus), Don Gray (Fairbanks), Fred Green (Orlando), Carole L. Hahn (Atlanta), Theodore Kaltsounis (Seattle), Charles L. Mitsakos (Boston), Douglas A. Phillips (Anchorage), Donald O. Schneider (Athens), Jo Ann Sweeney (Austin), and Judith Torney-Purta (College Park).

In the 1970s, NCSS expanded its international activities beyond its strong publications program to direct involvement with social studies educators in other nations. The intellectual argument underlying this new direction was that, although social studies had become a transnational profession, social studies practitioners in the United States knew very little about what was happening in the profession elsewhere and seemed, in fact, to be practicing a self-imposed isolation. The social studies profession itself had become part of the global village, and NCSS became an active player. Implicitly, it was assumed that this participation would indirectly improve classroom instruction in social studies in all participating nations.

These fresh NCSS efforts included:
- Cosponsoring international meetings with organizations like UNESCO and the Bundeszentrale für Politische Bildung;
- Sponsoring professional development travel/study programs; and
- Incorporating international educators into

the NCSS annual meeting as presenters and into its publications as major authors.

1976: UNESCO and NCSS

In May 1976, a group of fourteen experts from nations around the world met in East Lansing, Michigan, to consider ways of strengthening the contribution of social studies to education for peace and respect for human rights. The meeting was sponsored by the United Nations Education, Science, and Cultural Organization (UNESCO) in cooperation with NCSS and the United States National Commission for UNESCO.

Stanley P. Wronski, then professor of social studies education at Michigan State University and past President of NCSS, organized the meeting. Howard D. Mehlinger, who was professor of history and education and director of the Social Studies Development Center at Indiana University, as well as President-elect of NCSS, was elected to chair the meeting.

The exchange of views and sharing of ideas produced a number of areas of consensus such as:

- social studies can and should play a significant role in education for international understanding, peace, and respect for human rights; and
- there is a great and immediate need to improve and expand social studies education in the primary and secondary school and in teacher-training programs.

An outgrowth of the meeting was the 1981 publication *UNESCO Handbook for the Teaching of Social Studies* (Mehlinger 1981). UNESCO and the U.S. National Commission for UNESCO helped bring NCSS into the global village in the late 1970s. This promising window to the world ended abruptly, however, with the election of Ronald Reagan as President in 1980—followed soon thereafter by the withdrawal of the United States from UNESCO and the dismantling of the U. S. National Commission by the U. S. State Department.

I served on the U.S. National Commission for UNESCO as the NCSS representative from 1977 to 1983, spanning the Jimmy Carter years and most of the first administration of Ronald Reagan. I thus witnessed the heavy-handed destruction of the Commission by the Reagan political appointees to the State Department and to the Commission, including William J. Bennett, then chairman of the National Endowment for the Arts and soon to become secretary of education.

Frankly, even today it is hard to believe what happened. The death of the Commission was painful. Loyal and faithful State Department officers put their careers on the line to save the Commission only to find themselves quickly forced out. It was an object lesson in the brutality of Washington politics. It should be noted that this is the same neoconservative grouping that dogged the social studies and global education throughout the 1980s and expanded its power in Congress significantly in the 1994 elections.

1977: Japan Study Tour Fellowship Program

Led by the late Charles von Loewenfeldt, the founder of the Japan Fellowship Program and a consultant with Japan Airlines and the Japanese government, the first group of NCSS members was invited to Japan in summer 1977 as a test case to investigate whether or not such a program were desirable and, if it were, who would fund it. The answer to the first question was "yes." When the second question was discussed, those on the Japan side agreed to underwrite the program. With funding first from The Japan Foundation and then from Keizai Koho (Japan Institute for Social and Economic Affairs), this remarkably vibrant project has functioned successfully for nearly twenty years. More than six hundred educators from the United States, Canada, and

Australia have participated in the annual study tours. Teachers from each state and each Canadian province have traveled to Japan and returned to develop classroom materials about Japan and its global role, especially its relationship with the United States.

The positive impact of the Japan Fellowship project on NCSS and the social studies profession in the United States would be difficult to overestimate. The confidence and the enthusiasm it engendered among members of NCSS helped lay the foundation for further NCSS international program development in the 1980s and 1990s.

In December 1986, a subcommittee of the NCSS International Activities Committee (IAC) met in Washington, D.C., to select the first group of NCSS members to participate in the Japan program. As the newly appointed chair of the IAC, I chaired the selection process. Our subcommittee could not have predicted the long-range impact of the program, but even then we sensed its potential for NCSS, and memories of this meeting remain vivid today.

Akio Nakajima, then cultural attaché in the Embassy of Japan and the originator of the idea, along with von Loewenfeldt, invited the subcommittee to his home in suburban Washington for dinner. He described how concerned the Japanese government was that the younger generation in the United States had little or no knowledge about Japan and were apathetic, at best, about his nation. This attitude was in contrast to the positive attitudes of their parents, who had learned about Japan during the post-World War II occupation.

Our host related that he and von Loewenfeldt had decided it was time to design a program to bring social studies teachers to Japan from the United States to help them teach American youngsters to be more knowledgeable about and favorable toward Japan. We found it especially interesting and admirable that the Japanese had used well-known polling organizations in the United States to obtain information on a periodic and systematic basis about American attitudes and images of Japan.

Years later, von Loewenfeldt recalled how he and Nakajima had walked apprehensively into the office of Brian Larkin, executive director of NCSS, and made their presentation. Then, Larkin replied, "Why not?" It was the right program at the right time.

1977: Social Studies in Other Nations

A few readers may recall a special event that took place during the NCSS annual meeting in Cincinnati in 1977. A plenary panel of social studies educators from Japan, Nigeria, Thailand, the United Kingdom, and West Germany addressed the audience on the subject of "Social Studies and Citizen Education: A Multinational Approach." The participants made presentations on social studies in their respective nations and on the relationship of social studies to citizenship education, the theme of the meeting. The session generated so much interest that the papers were later brought together in an NCSS bulletin *Teaching Social Studies in Other Nations* (Mehlinger and Tucker 1978).

This session and its subsequent publication both reflected and encouraged the growing interest within NCSS in the profession of social studies around the world. A special interest group was established in NCSS called the International Exchange for Social Studies. In the late 1970s and early 1980s, this informal group worked closely with the more formally structured NCSS International Activities Committee to sponsor presentations by social studies educators from other countries on the program of the annual meeting and to make foreign guests comfortable at the meeting. These and other activities were all part of a conscious effort by NCSS and individual members to reach out to educators around the world.

However, these efforts, intermittently successful, failed to permeate the consciousness of the organization and membership overall. Several reasons help explain this failure. At this time, NCSS was experiencing serious internal problems and having trouble meeting its financial obligations. It did not help that the executive director who resigned during that period was closely identified with international activities. Of greatest significance, nevertheless, was the 1980 election of Ronald Reagan—ushering in a completely new national agenda, unfavorable to international education.

The 1980s: The Global Village and NCSS under Siege

By the beginning of the 1980s, NCSS had surely entered the global village. Indeed, in many ways, the Council was a leader among educational organizations, but international events and domestic politics combined to create an extremely negative climate for global studies. The Soviet Union invaded Afghanistan in late 1979, and President Carter withdrew the United States from the 1980 Olympic Games held in Moscow. Later that year, Ronald Reagan was elected president partly because of his promise to restore respect for American might around the world; a few years later he famously described the Soviet Union as the "evil empire."

The Cold War had reached a new level. Although the period was confusing and frustrating for international and global educators, they tried to dig in and hold onto their progress. In spite of their attempts, however, international activities were marginalized by the NCSS Board of Directors, largely through benign neglect, as other issues loomed, such as a social studies curriculum scope and sequence.

The climate shifted rapidly from stifling to threatening when in 1986 the Denver regional office of the U.S. Department of Education launched an inquiry into the quality of the classroom materials produced and sold by the Center for Teaching International Relations (CTIR) at the University of Denver. The report "Blowing the Whistle on Global Education" (Cunningham 1986), widely circulated among educators, accused CTIR and global educators in general of fostering a moral relativism that accepts any single social, economic, and political system as morally indistinguishable from any other.

NCSS established an ad hoc committee on global education to inquire into the Denver situation and report to the Board of Directors. The committee, chaired by Stanley P. Wronski, published its report in the April/May 1987 issue of *Social Education* under the title of "Global Education: In Bounds or Out?" (Wronski 1987). The committee's report criticized the procedures and findings of the Denver study and went on to recommend standards for global education materials and programs.

Despite the end of the Cold War in the late 1980s, many of the issues of that period are still with us, and some of the major players are still active. The 1996 presidential campaign probably will see a sequel to that period, played out this time against a backdrop of the alleged decline of moral virtues and family values.

I witnessed the comparative decrease of NCSS interest in international activities in the early 1980s from two vantage points: as the appointed NCSS representative to the U.S. National Commission for UNESCO and as an elected member of the NCSS Board of Directors, serving from 1980 to 1982. Ted Kaltsounis, President of NCSS in 1981, attempted to influence the Board of Directors to consider changing the name of NCSS to "International Council for the Social Studies." While only a few years earlier this proposal had been discussed among NCSS members as a reasonable idea, it was hooted down by the Board and treated as a ludicrous notion.

Elliot Abrams, then Assistant Secretary of State for International Organizations and a tough opponent of UNESCO and the U.S. National Commission for UNESCO, made a special effort to discredit the international human rights programs and publications that had only recently been coproduced by NCSS and the National Commission. In a major speech during the 1983 NCSS Annual Meeting in San Francisco, he attacked NCSS Bulletin No. 68, *International Human Rights, Society, and the Schools* (Branson and Torney-Purta 1982), partially funded by the U.S. National Commission, for not emphasizing human rights violations within communist nations, especially the Soviet Union.

To put it mildly, this attack by a ranking member of the U.S. State Department on NCSS for being soft on communism had a chilling effect on the Council's leadership and membership. How things had changed within a five-year period! It was at once breathtaking and demoralizing for this blitzkrieg to be launched at both the U.S. National Commission for UNESCO and NCSS.

The 1990s: NCSS Regroups

By the late 1980s, NCSS had shaken off its self-imposed slowdown on international activities. In no small measure, this new life was due to the end of the Cold War. Freed from shrill Cold War charges by conservative academicians and politicians, NCSS began to sponsor international programming that ranged from travel/study tours to international conferences. For example, the Board included in its long-range planning the sponsorship of an international conference on social studies on a three-year cycle. To date, such conferences have been held successfully in Vancouver (1988), Miami (1991), and Nairobi (1994). The next such conference is scheduled for Australia in 1997.

The idea of holding regular international conferences on the social studies sprang from a discussion over coffee between Don Wilson (Vancouver) and me during the 1985 annual meeting in Chicago. The fact that Wilson offered Vancouver as a site for the first international meeting enabled me, as NCSS Vice-President at the time, with the help of Margit McGuire and others, to convince the Board that the idea was viable. Lifetime friendships have been sealed and international communication about social studies increased exponentially as a result of these conferences.

In 1994, following protracted discussions over several years, the NCSS Board of Directors established the International Assembly. It has the same status within NCSS as, for example, the College and University Faculty Assembly. The inaugural meeting, under the chairmanship of Robert H. Fowler (Canada), was held during the 1994 annual meeting in Phoenix.

Despite these positive changes, tensions between the domestic role of NCSS and the challenges of the global village will create contentious issues into the foreseeable future. Most NCSS members are classroom teachers in the United States, who must account at the local level each day for their performance. They are pinched between immediate and powerful local demands, often created by conservative political forces, and the longer range, but equally exacting changes caused by the events and pressures of the rapidly developing global village.

The global forces will intensify. It will not be business as usual for NCSS. If, for example, the centrality of the nation-state itself is in decline, as some writers like Paul Kennedy (1991) have suggested, the conventional theory of social studies based on citizenship education itself will come under increasing scrutiny.

NCSS members and leaders of the next seventy-five years, however, can proceed in the difficult work ahead with assurance that their predecessors have built a solid foundation.

References

Anderson, L. *Schooling and Citizenship in a Global Age.* Bloomington, Ind.: The Mid-America Program for Global Perspectives in Education, 1979.

Becker, J. M., ed. *Schooling for a Global Age.* New York: McGraw-Hill, 1979.

Becker, J. M., and H. D. Mehlinger, eds. *International Dimensions in the Social Studies. 38th Yearbook.* Washington, D.C.: National Council for the Social Studies, 1968.

Branson, M. S., and J. Torney-Purta. *International Human Rights, Society, and the Schools.* Bulletin 68. Washington, D.C.: National Council for the Social Studies, 1982.

Carson, R. *Silent Spring.* Boston: Houghton-Mifflin, 1962.

Cunningham, G. L. "Blowing the Whistle on Global Education." Paper prepared for Thomas G. Tancredo, Secretary's Regional Representative, Region VIII (Denver Office), U. S. Department of Education, 1986.

Ehrlich, P. R. *The Population Bomb.* New York: Ballantine, 1968.

Fuller, R. B. *Operating Manual for Spaceship Earth.* New York: Pocket Books, 1970.

Hanvey, R. *Developing a Global Perspective.* New York: Center for Global Perspectives in Education (The American Forum for Global Education), 1976.

Kennedy, P. *Preparing for the Twenty-First Century.* New York: Random House, 1991.

LaFeber, W. "We Need Fresh Scholarship to Understand Changed World Realities." *The Chronicle of Higher Education* 35 (May 24, 1989): A40.

Long, H. M., and R. N. King. *Improving the Teaching of World Affairs: The Glens Falls Story.* Bulletin 35. Washington, D.C.: National Council for the Social Studies, 1964.

McLuhan, M. *Understanding Media: The Extensions of Man.* New York: McGraw-Hill, 1964.

Meadows, D. H., D. L. Meadows, J. Randers, and W. W. Behrens III. *The Limits to Growth: A Report for the Club of Rome's Project on the Predicament of Mankind.* New York: Universe Books, 1972.

Mehlinger, H. D., ed. *UNESCO Handbook for the Teaching of Social Studies.* London: Croom Helm, 1981.

Mehlinger, H. D., and J. L. Tucker, eds. *Teaching Social Studies in Other Nations.* Bulletin 60. Washington, D.C.: National Council for the Social Studies, 1978.

Natoli, S. J., ed. *James A. Michener on the Social Studies: His Writings in Publications of National Council for Social Studies from 1938 to 1987.* Bulletin 85. Washington, D.C.: National Council for the Social Studies, 1991.

Nesbitt, W. A., ed. "International Education for the Twenty-First Century." *Social Education* 35, no. 7 (1968): 637-92.

Remy, R. C., J. A. Nathan, J. M. Becker, and J. V. Torney. *International Learning and International Education in a Global Age.* Bulletin 47. Washington, D.C.: National Council for the Social Studies, 1978.

Stavrianos, L. S. *Lifelines from Our Past: A New World History.* New York: Pantheon, 1989.

Teilhard de Chardin, P. *Future of Man.* Translated by N. Denny. New York: Harper & Row, 1964.

Thomas, L. *The Lives of a Cell: Notes of a Biology Watcher.* New York: Viking Press, 1974.

Toffler, A. *Future Shock.* New York: Random House, 1970.

Ward, B., and R. Dubos. *Only One Earth: The Care and Maintenance of a Small Planet.* New York: Norton, 1972.

Wronski, S. P., J. E. Fair, R. K. Fullinwider, and R. L. Boyes. "Report of the Ad Hoc Committee on Global Education." *Social Education* 51, no. 4 (1987): 242-49.

NCSS *and Ethnic/Cultural Diversity*

**Jesus Garcia and
Edward Buendia**
University of Illinois, Champaign

IT IS REPUTED THAT YOGI BERRA ONCE UTTERED THESE IMMORTAL words, "Here it is, déjà vu all over again!" Many of us in the educational community find the phrase appropriate when describing change in education.

Consider the issue of textbook-dominated instruction in secondary classrooms. Was this a "cutting edge" issue a few decades ago? A decade ago? Is it an issue today? Have secondary classrooms become less textbook driven since researchers brought this issue to the attention of teachers? To us, the manner in which individuals respond to these questions is less dependent on the number of years they have spent in the field of education than on their insights about the ability of public education to initiate, implement, and sustain change. Many of us who have devoted a considerable part of our professional lives to public education and attended more than a few national education meetings have formed some strong opinions about education and its ability to respond to change.

Professional educational organizations (e.g., National Council for the Social Studies, National Council of Teachers of English, International Reading Association, National Council of Teachers of Mathematics) are an integral part of the educational community. They play major roles in the initiation and sustenance of change. Among their many functions, they represent their respective teaching field to teachers and the public. In the educational community, they provide and nurture leadership, conduct and promote research, disseminate professional literature, introduce teachers to trends and issues in their particular subject areas, and bring to the forum of debate changes suggested by the membership, interest groups, and the general public. This article examines changes in the treatment of minorities and in the concept of cultural diversity in NCSS.

By examining the issue of minorities in NCSS, we stress the importance of social studies educators becoming more aware of the performance of their organization. Comments by social studies educators on the organization's performance level may lead to a better understanding of NCSS's interpretation of minority/cultural diversity issues within the context of social studies. We also believe that this investigation may provide the social studies community with more effective methods (e.g., position statements, definitions, publications) of integrating the work of NCSS with the teaching of social studies and cultural diversity. As members of the organization— one relatively new, and the other active for the past two decades—we believe that we offer colleagues a "minority perspective" on how the organization is perceived by an admittedly small segment of its membership. On a broader note, we also believe that NCSS is similar to other organizations, in that change initiated and sustained by the leadership is extremely difficult, and even when it is initiated, it is sometimes imperceptible to the public.

Our goal is threefold: (1) to examine the treatment of minority-related issues in NCSS; (2) to examine the role of minorities in NCSS; and (3) to identify bureaucratic responses by the organization (membership, staff, officers, organizational structure) to complement its official position on cultural diversity. We addressed these three goals by reading House of Delegates (HOD) minutes; studying the organization's policy and committee manuals; reviewing *Social Education*, NCSS's major publication; and interviewing past elected officials of NCSS and national office staff. We focused on a thirty-four year time period (1960-1994).

In this investigation, we used the term "cultural diversity" rather than "minorities" because we believe that the phrase is more inclusive: it refers both to minorities and other groups who have been identified as marginalized in NCSS, and it refers to issues relating to cultural diversity as an intellectual concept. The broadness of the phrase also enabled us to capture definitional and operational changes over time. We considered such questions as, What did "cultural diversity" mean in the 1960s? What does it mean today? Does NCSS interpret the phrase "cultural diversity" to mean issues relating only to traditional minority groups (i.e., Native Americans, African Americans, Asian Americans, and Hispanics)? What was the organization's ethnic membership composition in the 1960s? What is it today? How has NCSS changed structurally over this thirty-four year period? Has the organization's mode of operation related to this issue changed over time?

NCSS House of Delegates

Since its beginnings seventy-five years ago, NCSS's record on the identification and treatment of issues relating to cultural diversity can best be characterized as deliberate and conservative. Prior to the 1960s, little discussion apparently occurred within the organization concerning the issue of diversity. For the time period of 1960-1990, we selected five-year intervals to examine the HOD minutes appearing in *Social Education*. In 1960 and 1965, issues relating to minorities do not appear in the minutes. In 1970, HOD passed two resolutions on the subject. One urged NCSS to "include among its priority goals those dealing with instructional programs concerning the Mexican-American"; the other urged NCSS to "develop a series of workshops for the next annual meeting to investigate the historical and contemporary role of women in creating not only equality for women but a new society." The first resolution passed but the second failed. The topic of cultural diversity does not appear in the 1975 minutes. In 1980, the HOD passed a resolution on "the detrimental effects of the Nestle formula on Third World Children," and in 1985, it passed a resolution "condemning apartheid in South Africa."

In the 1990s, the HOD passed a number of resolutions that could be construed as addressing issues relating specifically to minorities and the concept of cultural diversity. In 1990, the HOD supported the findings of the Task Force on Membership and Participation of Minorities in NCSS by passing the following resolution: "Be it resolved that the House of Delegates urge state and local councils to support the NCSS goal of inclusion of all groups through the development of action programs in their state and local councils." In 1992, it passed a resolution "concerning the composition of NCSS committees and committee chairs" and another on "age, gender, sexual orientation, race, ethnicity, and religious intolerance." In 1993, it commended "Each One, Reach One," a committee designed to increase NCSS membership, but it failed to pass a resolution sponsored by the Equity and Social Justice Committee that it remain a standing committee in NCSS. It also passed a resolution regarding the Washington Redskins, a professional football team in the National Football League: "Be it resolved that NCSS condemns the continued use of such names [Redskins] and encourages its members to boycott games, products, and anything else associated with this and other similar organizations until such times as these oppressive names and accompanying logos are changed."

NCSS Publications and Cultural Diversity

Prior to the 1960s, articles focusing on cultural diversity in the organization's journal, *Social Education*, were almost non-existent (Chapin and Gross 1970). The few articles appearing during that time period focused on the distorted portrayal of African Americans in the social studies curriculum. Such was the theme of John Hope Franklin's essay in which he urged the publishing industry to provide learners with a historically accurate depiction of African Americans and to move away from distortions and sweeping overgeneralizations (Franklin 1950). Franklin's appeal for cultural and historical accuracy would remain the prevailing theme until the late 1960s. Other social studies researchers writing during this time would pursue the treatment of marginalized groups in social studies by addressing the following question: "What attention should be given to minority groups in the social studies curriculum?" (Kenworthy 1968, 483).

Using the issues of *Social Education* that included the HOD minutes, we examined the tables of contents for articles that described minority concerns and issues relating to cultural diversity. (Because a part of this issue of *Social Education* includes records of NCSS annual meeting business, the number of articles appearing in the journal was less than the normal number.) In the 1961 and 1966 issues, no articles were found, but the March 1971 issue carried two such articles, one addressing women in U.S. history textbooks and the other Native American participation in education. In the February 1976 issue of *Social Education*, an article highlighted children's trade books on Irish, Italian, and Polish Americans; so too did the NCSS *Curriculum Guidelines on Multicultural Education*. No articles appeared in the 1981 issue; in 1986, an article appeared titled "Blacks and Hispanics in High School Economics Texts."

No relevant articles appeared in the April/May 1991 issue of *Social Education*. There were two articles in the April/May 1992 issue: "Multicultural/Global Education: An Educational Agenda for the Rights of the Child" and "Choosing Materials for Teaching about the Columbian Quincentenary." In 1993, two articles appeared: one a reply to the NCSS Columbus Quincentenary Statement and the other on immigration to Europe. No relevant articles appeared in the April/May 1994 issue of *Social Education*.

The writings of James A. Banks, a past President of NCSS, have been identified in *Social Education* issues as particularly influential in the discussion of issues of diversity in social studies education. Many of the early articles reflect Banks's thinking in the area of cultural diversity. While the educational community was employing terms such as "culturally disadvantaged" and "culturally deprived," Banks's work first examined the treatment of African Americans in textbooks and then moved quickly into the area of ethnic studies. Initially, Banks envisioned an inquiry-driven social studies program that would enable African American students to learn about themselves and their historical contributions to the United States and the world. He further held that through inquiry skills, students would "be guided to inquire in the problems of racial discrimination, institutional racism, the meaning and social functions of race, and the struggle that ensues when one race dominates others in a society" (Banks 1969, 67). In the late 1960s, Banks introduced the phrase "ethnic studies" and began a discussion on issues relating to African Americans that, in time, would give rise to the phrase "multicultural education" (a discussion of issues relating to minority and white ethnic groups).

In the 1970s, 1980s, and 1990s, Banks and others expanded their focus beyond racial and ethnic groups. Some elevated the concept to a global level and argued for units of study that were issue-oriented, multi-level, and interdisciplinary in nature. Thus, in a period of three decades, minority studies had moved from a single group study to an examination of a variety of groups based on the intellectual concept of cultural diversity. Many have applauded this evolution of ethnic studies in the social studies, i.e., an inclusionary model identifying a wide range of social groups (local, national, international) as part of multicultural education. Others, however, believe that the change has resulted in a shift in attention from issues commonly associated with social studies and traditional minority groups.

The articles we identified in *Social Education* indicate that NCSS has been following the evolution of multicultural education and has published articles that address both theory and application. In addition, a cursory look at articles appearing in issues of *Social Education* and in bulletins and yearbooks suggests that NCSS has explored a number of issues relating to minorities and cultural diversity. In fact, one of NCSS's most recent publications, the reprint of the *Guidelines on Multicultural Education*, underscores the organization's commitment to cultural diversity.

NCSS Elected Officials and Staff

When we selected for interview staff members in the NCSS national office in Washington, D.C., and former elected NCSS officials, we told them that we were writing an article for the Council's 75th Anniversary commemorative bulletin. We explained that we were seeking personal perceptions of the organization's inclusion of minorities and the treatment of minority and cultural diversity issues. All the persons with whom we spoke asserted that they believed NCSS was committed to the following: (1) integrating the experiences of minorities and other cultural groups into the social studies curriculum; (2) recruiting minorities into the organization; and (3) speaking out against individuals and organizations preaching hatred and intolerance of minorities and other social groups.

The individuals we interviewed cited the following evidence to substantiate their conclusions: the establishment of ad hoc committees on membership and the issue of underrepresented groups in the organization;

progress in diversifying the composition of NCSS advisory committees; an increased number of programs on cultural diversity topics and speakers of minority backgrounds at annual meetings; active efforts to encourage minorities to seek national office; and publication of articles relating social studies to minority issues. As the leaders remarked, there is no lack of creative ideas!

In our interviews, NCSS officials offered a number of examples of what they described as NCSS's spirited leadership in providing the social studies community with theoretical models and strategies on how best to present the experiences of minority groups in the social studies. Some of those examples are included in this chapter. However, these same individuals said much less about initiatives by the organization regarding how best to provide for those learners from minority backgrounds who experience difficulties in social studies classrooms. Few discussed the status of social studies in our nation's inner cities, the dwindling numbers of minority teachers, or the best ways to provide social studies instruction to new immigrants and minority youth.

On a related subject, a constant source of frustration to NCSS officials is the slow pace of organizational change. According to many former and current NCSS leaders, both the national and local councils are slow to initiate change that would disturb the status quo or require additional work on the part of individuals, the majority of whom are volunteer leaders.

Some of these individuals suggested that some NCSS members were "uneasy" discussing issues that could result in leadership change within the social studies community. Nevertheless, NCSS staff members felt positive about ideas that had come out of the resolutions, committee recommendations, and suggestions from the Board of Directors, executive directors, and Presidents. However, some believed that many of the recommendations would "stay on the shelf" because sufficient human and financial resources were not available to carry out the wishes of the organization. One individual provided a rather critical interpretation of the suggestions emanating from NCSS's bureaucratic structure: "NCSS members use the HOD as the forum to pass resolutions and support committee recommendations addressing what they call the 'minority problem,' knowing these initiatives will have little impact at the state and local levels. These members merely want to leave the national meeting each year knowing they have expressed their concern on minority issues."

Individuals with whom we spoke generally agreed that multicultural education/cultural diversity as an intellectual issue was being addressed by the organization. However, they felt that dialogue about minority teachers and students and social studies education was minimal, at best, and that little progress, if any, had occurred regarding inclusion of minorities within the organizational framework of NCSS and its affiliates. Most individuals, however, were optimistic and believed that, while change in the last two areas was not significant, progress was occurring. They believed that NCSS's national headquarters was doing the very best that it could in these two areas. The commitment was present. Absent were the resources and a leadership style that included greater risk taking.

Personal Observations

In the examination of issues relating to cultural diversity, pointing a finger and screaming "fire" may be too easy a response. We believe that these issues are far too complex to be reduced to finger-pointing and emotionally charged phrases. Calling for attacks on "the establishment," "white middle-class America," and "those racist forces out to undermine progress in the area of cultural diversity and social studies education" does not help to create an atmosphere in which an open discussion may occur on issues that affect all social studies educators. After examining the evidence and applying our own perspectives to the evidence, we offer our analysis of the status of minorities and minority issues in NCSS. However, before addressing the questions we posed in this paper, each NCSS member should recognize that we are viewing not only an organization, but also the educators who comprise the organization. These are two different phenomena, for the behavior and actions of an organization are not the same as those of many individuals or small groups within it.

Like other organizations, NCSS plays a number of roles. However, we believe that the primary role of NCSS is to promote social studies to the greater educational community, to national politicians and officials, and to the many interest groups that want to know what constitutes social studies in American public schools. In this role, NCSS wishes to promote ideas that are acceptable to those groups that have the power to affect social studies in public education.

One way the organization promotes social studies is through its publications. *Expectations of Excellence: Curriculum Standards for Social Studies*, a recent NCSS publication, is both an excellent document for education and an effective promotional tool because it defines social studies and describes how to create exemplary social studies programs. Embedded in the document, although not highlighted, are issues relating to cultural diversity as an intellectual concept. At the 1994 annual meeting, the contents of the document sparked many discussions. We suspect that this document will continue to be cited and presented to the public as an example of the work of NCSS. We also believe that when non-members read *Expectations of Excellence: Curriculum Standards for Social Studies*, they too will support the organization's definition of social studies and the teaching of social studies.

Although NCSS has responded to the challenge of dealing with issues of minorities and cultural diversity, it has done so in a deliberate way, reflecting the organization's conservatism. Having attended a number of national, state, and local meetings, we have concluded that the majority of the members who attend NCSS conferences are white males and females. (NCSS members are not obligated to report race or ethnic identification; the data available from the national office can be characterized as "ballpark" figures.) However, what makes the membership conservative is not race, ethnicity, or gender but the professional positions of NCSS members and their places of work and residence. Most appear to be elementary and secondary school teachers, state directors of social studies, local curriculum leaders, or college professors, mostly from a middle-class, professional environment. Many of the members are well versed on issues relating to minorities and cultural diversity. However, although describing a culturally diverse America and preparing students to live in a culturally pluralistic world are issues of primary importance to them, they appear to be less concerned about the issues of teaching minorities in the inner cities, increasing the number of minority teachers in social studies, building social studies programs in inner cities, or changing the racial complexion of NCSS. Given the general characteristics of the membership—their topical background, academic training, and place of employment—the relative lack of attention to issues relating to minorities and cultural diversity seems easy to understand.

Given the make-up of the membership, we are not surprised that a conservative ideology dominates NCSS. However, adhering to a particular ideology is not without its weaknesses. In this instance, conservativism does not (1) promote the inclusion of a cross-section of America's social studies teachers; (2) initiate, develop, and sustain good social studies in all kinds of community—rural, urban, and suburban; and (3) support risk-taking initiatives aimed at developing good social studies for the inner-city student. The present diversity of NCSS membership seems insufficient to provide for an open and critical examination of many of the issues associated with American minority groups and cultural diversity. In our opinion, the general membership simply does not see minority issues as we have described them in this paper.

Perhaps a more diversified membership would offer a different set of priorities. But would a more culturally diverse membership result in a more liberal NCSS agenda? And would a less conservative NCSS be acceptable to most American social studies teachers and the larger educational community?

Through its publications, NCSS has adequately treated an array of issues relating to cultural diversity and minorities. A diverse group of scholars is writing in the area; practical suggestions, sustained by theory, are available to elementary and secondary teachers; and one result of their attention is sustained progress in integrating diverse content in social studies programs. Recently, for example, *Social Education* has published special issues on the "United Nations" and "Women in Wartime" and such articles as "American Indians as Economic Decision Makers," "The Challenge of Social Studies for Limited English Proficient Students," "Making Every Picture Count: Ethnicity in Primary Grade Textbook Photographs," and "Africa: Myth and Reality."

Nevertheless, while NCSS has made significant contributions in this area, some issues seem to be overlooked. They include (1) the status of social studies in urban and rural areas, (2) the dwindling number of social studies teachers who are of minority background, and (3) the quality of social studies instruction in schools and classrooms composed predominantly of individuals from traditional minority

groups. In a nation and world that are increasingly multicultural, in which young women and men of minority groups populate urban centers and are beginning to migrate to suburban America, and in which educational change in the inner cities moves at a snail's pace, these issues should not be left to chance. They should be major research and action issues. Moreover, we believe that a critical examination of these issues would invariably lead to recommendations in the areas of pedagogy and social studies, the role of diversity in the teaching of social studies, and the role of NCSS in promoting high-quality social studies for all learners. How would the leadership of NCSS react to recommendations calling for drastic changes in the composition of its membership and its non-elected leadership? Would the organization pursue these recommendations with state and local councils? Would the interests of NCSS be served in the serious pursuit of these recommendations? Does NCSS possess the structure and the resources to pursue such initiatives?

Another way of looking at these questions and what we have labeled the conservative nature of NCSS is to examine the resolutions passed by the HOD and those cited in this paper. One set of the recommendations focused on national and global issues, e.g., apartheid, racism, big business, and third world countries. The recommendations from two ad hoc committees, which also became resolutions, focused on membership, e.g., encouraging elementary teachers, minorities, and urban teachers to join NCSS. These recommendations address a number of issues and problems and provide the Board of Directors with an opportunity to identify a variety of strategies aimed at changing NCSS. All of the resolutions are noteworthy because they underscore the organization's sensitivity to issues relating to minorities and cultural diversity. However, passage of the resolutions without subsequent action makes them public relations statements aimed merely at informing the general educational community that NCSS is informed and aware of local and global issues, sensitive to the problems plaguing humankind, and seeming to act on obstacles that prevent the organization from meeting its goals.

Another way of viewing the resolutions passed by the HOD is to focus on the action called for in them. For example, the resolutions on "Nestle formula," "the Redskins," and "apartheid" called for the membership to condemn the actions of individuals, groups, and countries, but they did not call for NCSS to expend human or financial resources. They asked each NCSS member to make a personal decision on racism and the plight of third world countries. As such, these "no risk" resolutions keep NCSS in line with other education and social science organizations, but they do not commit NCSS resources or suggest changes in the manner in which the organization conducts its day-to-day business. In addition to condemning apartheid, NCSS could have launched a public relations campaign along with other education associations and, for example, have lobbied education-oriented establishments to refrain from doing business with South Africa. This example underscores a flaw in NCSS governance structure and highlights why the Council likely would not pursue such a campaign. Put simply, the organization does not possess the power or resources to undertake such a campaign. Moving the 1994 Annual Meeting from Denver to Phoenix because of Colorado's position on gay issues placed NCSS in the mainstream with other organizations; this was not a high-risk decision. Similarly, the resolution urging "state and local councils to support the NCSS goal of inclusion of all groups through the development of action programs in their state and local councils" had the potential to influence the organization, but the NCSS governance structure limits the organization's power to

that of persuasion. That is, NCSS can only make suggestions and urge state and local councils, but it cannot direct them how to conduct their business. Hence, the recommendations developed by the Ad Hoc Committee on Minorities and Other Underrepresented Groups—for instance, that "state and local councils actively recruit" and that there be "greater cooperation among the various education organizations to encourage more minority youth to consider teaching as a profession"—lost their impact when presented to the HOD and translated into a resolution.

In our opinion, if change is to occur in the NCSS membership and the manner in which Council business is conducted as it relates to traditional minority groups and, perhaps, other issues, one of two things must happen. First, the governance and structure of relations between local and state councils and the national council must change, or secondly, local and state councils must begin to take a more aggressive leadership role in shaping NCSS into a more inclusive organization. Changing the existing relationship among the councils would allow the Board of Directors, President, executive director, and national staff to exercise greater leadership in all areas of the social studies. More culturally diverse national and state councils would result in an HOD that was more sensitive to all issues relating to social studies, including the problems commonly associated with minorities and the inner cities. We believe that a grassroots approach would go far in establishing NCSS as an organization that promotes quality social studies for all learners.

Regardless of which strategy is taken, each approach raises some interesting questions. Would NCSS officers or the HOD be willing to assume a greater role in making decisions about social studies education? Would they take risks and perhaps assume unpopular but just positions in order to address systemic problems in NCSS, in local/state councils, and in social studies education generally? Are local and state councils willing to aggressively recruit and open their ranks to groups that have been marginalized from the social studies community? Is the leadership in state and local councils willing to share power?

The last issue we would like to address is the role of minorities in NCSS. To do so, we must pose a fundamental question: How many individuals who identify themselves as members of traditional minority groups are members of NCSS? What was the ethnic composition of the organization a decade ago? Three decades ago? What are the projections for the twenty-first century? A simple answer to all of these questions is that no one knows. NCSS membership forms do not require any information about a member's ethnicity or race. Hence, we can only guess at the number of individuals from traditional minority groups who are members of NCSS. Given what the national office presently requires of its membership, we wonder, for example, what the meaning was of the Board of Directors' acceptance of the recommendations of the Ad Hoc Committee on Underrepresented Groups and why the HOD urged "state and local councils to develop action plans." How did NCSS expect to change the organization if it could not accurately report figures on the racial or ethnic composition of the membership? We believe that the number of NCSS members who are African Americans is small and the numbers of those who are Hispanic, Native American, or Asian American is extremely small. However, the number of African Americans who attend annual meetings is sufficiently high that a Special Interest Group (SIG) has been established.

Many of us who are of a minority background ask two questions when we find ourselves in organizations composed primarily of white educators: Am I welcomed into the organization because of the color of my skin or because of my academic credentials? And am I

perceived as a minority social studies educator (someone who is perceived to be an expert, regardless of credentials, on all issues relating to minorities), or a social studies educator? Silly questions? Not really. Today, many school districts, community colleges, and colleges and universities search frantically for minority applicants to join their faculties. Some universities even reward departments with an additional tenure-track position when they are able to convince a minority person to join their faculty. At NCSS annual meetings, particularly when the discussion turns to issues of diversity, these questions routinely surface. They certainly become prominent when committee membership and speakers for state, regional, and annual meetings are being considered.

In the last 15 years, the authors of this paper have been involved in state, regional, and national NCSS meetings, but the comments that follow center on our experiences at national conferences. During this time period, we have interacted with other minority members, listened to their professional concerns, spoken with minorities on a social level, and served on a number of committees that can be characterized as culturally diverse and that have addressed issues relating to minorities. (Regardless of the level of intimacy we have established with our minority colleagues, this chapter does not claim to articulate an "official" minority voice of NCSS. Rather, it presents our interpretation of what we have heard and experienced as a result of those interactions.) Our objective in the next few paragraphs is not to "sound preachy" or to lecture, but instead to illustrate the quality of the interaction between NCSS members who are white and those of color.

Many ethnic minority members feel that they are welcomed into NCSS to serve the organization's goals of enhancing diversity and not to truly address their concerns on matters relating to marginalized groups and social studies. Minorities wish to be perceived as social studies educators who are members of minority groups, and to be judged for their intellectual contributions to discussions relating to the social studies. They dislike being thought of as "quota makers" as the organization attempts to diversify itself. Many hold strong opinions about issues related to self-identification; they dislike intensely the fact that physical characteristics seem to overly influence how colleagues view them. For example, the authors of this paper are Hispanic, and we dislike the fact that some of our colleagues characterize us as bilingual, experts in bilingual education, and individuals who are privy to an "official position" on matters relating to Hispanics and social studies. On the other hand, we recognize that some other Hispanic members of NCSS have been academically trained in matters relating to minority issues and do possess the competence to speak on these issues.

Many minorities also dislike being cast in the role of "experts" because of what that role has done to the discussion on minority issues and cultural diversity. An incident involving the senior author of this paper should suffice to describe our feelings. A few years ago, I attended an NCSS committee meeting with a number of my white colleagues who, on numerous occasions but in other settings, have expressed to me their opinion on a number of issues including minorities, cultural diversity, and social studies. At this particular meeting, the group was quite vocal, with every member contributing to the discussion. However, when the committee moved to discuss a "minority" issue, a silence fell over the room and more than one person turned to me in expectation that I would issue the "official" minority position on the issue. Why did this happen? I do not know. Still, I believe that it is an example of "the culture of dealing with minority issues." Somehow, too many have adopted the following mistaken understandings: (1) Whites, irrespective of their qualifi-

cations, cannot speak on issues relating to minorities; (2) Whites, if they wish to avoid the label "racist," do not speak on issues associated with minorities; (3) Minorities are experts on minority issues because they are members of minority groups; and (4) Minority persons can become "overnight" experts because no one will challenge their positions on minority issues.

Today, as a result of fears of "political incorrectness," the atmosphere in some NCSS forums at which minority issues are discussed increasingly has become oppressive. Not only are certain terms and phrases understood to be taboo, but individuals (minority and non-minority) argue that research and discussion on minority issues can only be conducted by members of certain groups. We seriously wonder about the destination to which this form of discussion will lead us. More importantly, we wonder how such an atmosphere can possibly support us in helping "young people develop the ability to make informed and reasoned decisions for the public good as citizens of a culturally diverse, democratic society in an interdependent world," as official NCSS documents call us to do.

Conclusion

A number of years ago, the senior author of this paper joined a large College of Education where he was the only minority faculty member and the number of undergraduate and graduate students of minority background was extremely small. Each day when he walked into the College of Education building, he noticed how "white" the faculty and students were. He also noticed that, at 4:30 p.m. each week day, a group of African Americans would enter the building to clean the offices and public facilities. After watching this scene for a few months, he began to ask his white colleagues whether or not they were aware of anything "peculiar" that occurred each weekday at 4:30 p.m. No one knew what he was talking about. They did not notice that the faculty, except for him, was all white and that they did not "see" the African American maids (as they were called at that time) who would enter the building each day. He and his faculty never engaged in a meaningful conversation about minorities and cultural diversity.

References

Banks, James A. "Relevant Social Studies for Black Pupils." *Social Education* 33, no. 1 (January 1969): 66-69.

Chapin, June R., and Richard E. Gross. "A Barometer of the Social Studies: Three Decades of Social Education." *Social Education* 34, no. 8 (November 1970): 788-95.

Franklin, John H. "New Perspectives in American Negro History." *Social Education* 14, no. 5 (May 1950): 196-200.

Kenworthy, Leonard S. "Changing the Social Studies Curriculum: Some Guidelines and a Proposal." *Social Education* 32, no. 5 (May 1968): 481-86.

NCSS *and Teacher Education*

Margit E. McGuire
Seattle University

SINCE THE PUBLICATION OF *A NATION AT RISK* (1983), THE REPORT OF THE National Commission on Excellence in Education, schooling and the preparation of teachers for that task have been under scrutiny. Charges and counter charges have been exchanged about who is to blame for this state of affairs. Political rhetoric about how best to prepare teachers for the complex task of teaching has continued. Still, little progress has been made in fundamentally changing the preparation of teachers for the field of social studies. This state of affairs is well documented in Shaver's 1991 *Handbook of Research on Social Studies Teaching and Learning*.

Teaching social studies presents unique challenges. Passing on the cultural heritage of the society is one of the primary responsibilities of the social studies curriculum. To meet this responsibility, a social studies program should be focused on the acquisition of knowledge, skills related to understanding and using that knowledge, and values and dispositions that lead students to be fully participating members of society. Thus, policymakers, the media, and others in our society have a particular interest in what is taught in this area and how it is taught, especially in relation to controversial issues. Naturally, any topic in social studies has the potential to be controversial. The complexities of its agenda, the political dimensions, and the continuing debate in the field about what the goals are and how to achieve them have made social studies an educational minefield.

In this chapter, I will explore some of the current challenges of teacher preparation that arise from this state of affairs. I also offer suggestions of ways in which we can meet the challenges of teaching social studies in today's classrooms.

Integrating Curriculum and Educating for Civic Competence

One of the major issues the field must address is what social studies is. Brophy and Alleman (1993) believe that what is fundamental to good instruction and curriculum—and I would add, preparation of teachers—is a clear understanding of the purpose of teaching social studies. Yet educators expound multiple (and often conflicting or confusing) definitions and purposes regarding social studies education. This lack of clarity is particularly problematic for beginning teachers as they are faced with absorbing a broad knowledge of subject matter and the teaching/learning process, and applying that knowledge to the unique challenges of student teaching.

The National Council for the Social Studies (NCSS) in 1992 took a step forward by reaching consensus on a definition for social studies. The definition provides a clear direction for curriculum and instruction in the social studies:

Social studies is the integrated study of the social sciences and humanities to promote civic competence.

Within the school program, social studies provides coordinated, systematic study drawing upon such disciplines as anthropology, archaeology, economics, geography, history, law, philosophy, political science, psychology, religion, and sociology as well as appropriate content from the humanities, mathematics, and natural sciences.

The primary purpose of social studies is to help young people develop the ability to make informed and reasoned decisions for the public good as citizens of a culturally diverse, democratic society in an interdependent world. (NCSS 1993)

The definition is significant in two ways.

First, it recognizes the importance of an integrated curriculum, both in terms of pedagogy and in the natural connections of knowledge beyond the academics' often rigid constructs of the disciplines. While there may be merit in the advanced study of a particular field to organize knowledge into disciplines, this construct limits knowledge, skills, and dispositions that are essential to the field of social studies in schools. Further, as we better understand the pedagogy of the teaching/learning process, it appears that holistic, contextualized, and meaningful classroom activities demand an integrated curriculum. This approach is consistent with the learning principles outlined in *A Vision of Powerful Teaching and Learning in the Social Studies: Building Social Understanding and Civic Efficacy* (NCSS 1993): "Social studies teaching and learning is powerful when it is meaningful, integrative, value-based, challenging and active" (216).

Second, social studies education for civic competence demands an action-oriented curriculum. Thus, as one begins to organize a curriculum and daily lessons, it is essential to ask "To what end?" For example, how does the study of the Civil War help a young person become more civically competent? Without clear answers to this kind of question, social studies education will continue to be enmeshed in political rhetoric that undermines the fundamental value of social studies education. Without clear guidelines, the beginning teacher is at a distinct disadvantage.

If we could prepare our teachers to accomplish the goal of achieving civic competence for all young people in our nation's schools, our nation might look very different. If we were to do nothing more than increase the voting percentage in elections, the American society could change in very dramatic ways—ways that may or may not be predictable. However, working toward and possibly achieving such goals may in fact not be what the policymakers and others in our society want. Of course, it would not be "politically correct" to suggest that we do not want to increase civic competence, but groups can use other strategies that effectively deter such an increase. One is to undermine the role of social studies education and label it as "tot sociology." Another is to develop standards on a discipline-based model and correspondingly to call into question the goals and objectives of multicultural education.

The Realities of Today's Classrooms: A Personal Case Study

Given this state of affairs, those of us who are involved in the preparation of beginning teachers have an enormous challenge. My own reflections on the challenges facing beginning teachers have been sharply focused in the past several years by returning to classrooms to teach as have many of my colleagues. In some ways, going into someone else's classroom to teach provides a similar experience to student teaching and has helped clarify for me the modern realities of teacher preparation. In the spring of 1994, I organized my responsibilities at the university so that I could take a month to teach a sixth grade social studies class every day. I want to share this experience and my reflections about it as a way to examine some of the important challenges before us as teacher educators.

I had in mind a number of goals for teaching in this classroom:

- To experience first-hand an inner-city classroom with a large number of main-streamed children,
- To gain experience in teaching in a middle school setting,
- To work with the storyline strategy with middle school children, and
- To teach to the goal of civic competence as a social studies outcome.

The bottom line was, "Could I do what I was asking my beginning teachers to do?"

Quite honestly, I was anxious, especially after the teacher explained that this was one of the toughest classes he had ever had.

The teacher asked that I teach the topic of the Early People of Pacific Northwest Coast (McGuire and Schlick Noe 1994). The storyline strategy that I used is both a process for facilitating learning and a structure for organizing the curriculum. The strategy uses the basic components of a story—scene, characters, and plot—to organize curriculum into meaningful and memorable learning experiences. Through the process of creating a story, pupils tackle problems that require them to make use of their knowledge and skills. Thus, the students become involved in creating a place, making characters to live in that place, and addressing critical incidents that evolve through issues raised by the children and historical events that actually occurred.

Beginning to Teach: The Classroom Population

I began my first lesson with a brief description of the storyline strategy, then quickly moved into an introduction of the storyline topic by reading a description of the environment of the Pacific Northwest Coast. Based on the reading, students were to recall the geographical features described, the flora and fauna of the region, and the climate. Midway into the lesson, I realized that this class needed more than an oral discussion in order to be actively involved in the process. Thus, we quickly moved into the actual creation of a representation of the place described by constructing a frieze or mural. I demonstrated a technique for mountain-making as well as simple strategies for making other geographical features and the flora and fauna of the region. I then organized the class into four groups to construct the scene.

At first, some of the children were reluctant to make the various components of the frieze.

In order for the scene to come together as a cohesive unit, negotiation of the placement of the various geographical features was essential. I became aware that even though it was late in the school year, this class comprised a group of individuals who were disconnected from each other. This situation was due, in part, to its being a classroom in which children came and went with great frequency. I estimated that of a class of approximately twenty-five students, almost ten moved in or out in the month that I was there. Added to this problem was a gender imbalance, with only six females in the group of twenty-five. The level of absenteeism was high, and on only a few occasions were all the students present at one time.

This situation may have been unusual due to the student population and time of school year. Nevertheless, it reminded me that the movement of students is an ongoing and often overlooked problem of today's classrooms. Essential to well-managed classrooms in which meaningful learning can occur is a sense of community and belonging. This is particularly difficult to achieve in the kind of situation I experienced. Nevertheless, teachers commonly work in even less desirable situations and must seek ways to address these problems. How do we educate beginning teachers to build a sense of community in such classrooms while they also try new teaching strategies such as storyline?

Teaching: The Classroom Environment

During the next couple of days, students engaged in a number of activities regarding the place they created and, despite the lack of community, accomplished a number of activities successfully. Among other things, students brainstormed a list of what people would need to survive in an environment such as this one. They listed such things as food, clothing, shelter, religion, and government. This activity led to a series of questions including, What kind of food would be found in this environment? How would the climate and natural resources influence the kinds of shelter used? How would the environment affect what kind of clothing people would wear?

In the process of discussing these questions, another challenge became obvious. These students had been programmed to "give the right answer." The classroom teacher explained that he relied on a direct instruction approach as the dominant strategy in his class. Consequently, as students experienced the series of questions, they at first began by asking if their responses were correct. I responded by asking them, "What do you think?" The transition from trying to find "the teacher's right answer" to students' constructing their own answers to the questions was difficult for them. Some children clearly were uncomfortable with the change, some were eager for the change, and some simply tuned out my efforts.

For me, this experience shed new light on how we professors frequently call upon our students to introduce new strategies in classrooms. We fail to take into account the environments in which our student teachers are to attempt such tasks. Classrooms are undergoing great change: the regular teacher is playing a different role, a new teacher has taken over the class for only part of the school year, and this teacher is a novice. Add to this disequilibrium several other factors: the novice is expected to introduce new teaching and learning strategies in a classroom environment that may not be conducive to the use of such strategies, and the cooperating teacher may not share the same teaching philosophy or style and, consequently, may be unable to offer support. Again we must ask, How do we prepare student teachers and support them in meeting such challenges?

Teaching: Cooperative Learning

The next step in the storyline was to create

characters to live in this Northwest Coast environment. Since the students were seated at tables, I explained that each table would represent a family. Each group was to decide who would be the members of the family, and each student was to create one family character. I provided a model for making the characters and a biography guidesheet to assist students in thinking about each character's identity and background.

I thought the students would find this activity engaging and would enjoy making their characters and creating biographies. They did not. Students were uninterested and unable to negotiate with others of their table group to create families. Consequently, while they created a family for their own character, their family was not connected with the characters created by other members of the class except for two girls who were friends and whose characters were sisters. Once again, the ability to connect students and build a sense of community was diminished because of the particular circumstances of the class group.

This situation reminded me of the situation when my own students return from student teaching and discuss their attempts at cooperative learning, a strategy highly touted in our teacher preparation program. They consistently report that in classrooms in which the teacher has not placed a high priority on community and group work, it is almost impossible for the student teachers to introduce the cooperative learning strategy. There is simply not enough time to develop cooperative learning skills, given the limitations of student teaching, other curriculum priorities, and the cooperating teacher's possible lack of support for such an endeavor. Once again, the strategies that seem so vital to effective instruction in the college methods courses may not be readily accomplished in the field setting.

Teaching and Assessment

Once the storyline characters were made and biographies written, students introduced their characters, a few each day, to the entire class. The introductions served to motivate others who were lagging behind in making their characters. They enjoyed the introductions and were imaginative in creating interesting background events.

The characters revealed some of the issues with which these young adolescents were dealing in their own lives. Physical strength was a dominant theme, as were issues of power. Interestingly, gender roles were an important topic and a class session was devoted to students thinking and talking about why a long, long time ago gender roles were well defined. This discussion evolved naturally, was meaningful as it grew out of the lessons related to the early people of the Pacific Northwest Coast, and provided, I believe, deeper insights and understanding of gender roles of long ago as contrasted with gender roles of today.

While the discussion was rich and the class as a whole was engaged in the discussion, currently accepted methods of assessment would not adequately measure the student learning that occurred during this enlightening discussion. These are exactly the kinds of issues that need time and attention in today's classrooms. The storyline is an example of an environment in which the discussion and responses are meaningful. If we want to foster such learning, then what kinds of assessment do we support and explore with our own students? What mixed messages do they receive about what's important to teach and what's important to assess?

The Class and Ownership

The students decided that they needed a leader for their village. This decision arose because the two sister characters announced that they were the village leaders. The boys protested and said that the class needed to vote to decide who the leader would be. We discussed how it might have happened a long, long time ago in this culture, and various ideas were listed about how people became leaders.

The students invested much energy in this topic, perhaps because it was an issue that they had raised and that they owned. Two class periods were devoted to how leaders would be selected. After consideration of many different ideas, the decision was made to draw names out of a hat. One leader would be chosen, with two assistant leaders selected after the first one was chosen. This method was selected because students thought it would be the fairest.

Obviously, the people of the Pacific Northwest Coast did not select their leaders in this manner. However, to build a sense of ownership for the problem and its resolution, it seemed more important to allow the students to consider the various alternatives for selecting a leader, with their attendant advantages and disadvantages, than to impose the historically correct method of leadership selection. It is important to note, however, that follow-up activities included field trips to local museums, presentations by guest speakers, and student reports on a variety of topics related to the early people of this region. At this phase of the learning process, students acquired the context for examining the various topics and a point of comparison for their own efforts to construct understanding for that time and place. In teacher education, then, questions need to be raised about how we view knowledge, make use of that knowledge, and prioritize what is most important to know.

Meaningful Learning and Students

Students engaged in a number of other activities as the storyline developed, concluding with a village celebration planned by the students, then individual research about the early people of the Pacific Northwest Coast.

Two significant learning experiences occurred during the storyline. I asked a colleague to visit the classroom in the role of Captain Bering. This activity was significant in two important ways: all the students were fully engaged in the role-playing, and they explored issues of trading that were meaningful both from a personal and historical standpoint. Captain Bering brought tools, buttons, and beads, and traded art that the students had created based on the design elements of Northwest Coast art. Students discussed how the introduction of new items would change their culture, cause inequity among the people, and whether or not Captain Bering could be trusted. When the students realized that they had traded their artwork for the tools, buttons, and beads, they experienced buyer's remorse. They had given up their artwork and they were not sure they had made good trades. These discussions were lively, meaningful, and personal to the students. I think that these discussions significantly deepened the students' conceptual understanding of the trading process.

The other important learning experience began with the reading of a U.S. government edict ordering the students to move onto a reservation, to give up their way of life, to stop hunting and fishing, to send their children to boarding school, and to stop speaking their native language. For an hour, we debated the moral and ethical issues involved. The students were outraged that the U.S. government could make such demands. At the beginning of this storyline, students could not discuss a topic for more than fifteen minutes, but at this point, the discussion lasted a full hour. When the lunch bell rang, the debate continued as students made their way to the lunchroom. Pupils articulated the issues and options available to them, which included moving away, going to war, or dying, rather than moving onto the reservation.

I believe that this discussion developed empathy for the native people's reservation experience and a critical view of federal government actions. In my view, this learning experience was perhaps the most important of the entire unit, although I realize that in other contexts, this topic may create anxiety because of its sensitivity. Further, to call into question the actions of the U.S. government in some communities is very controversial. I believe, however, that these are important topics in the social studies curriculum. How can we begin to develop civically competent students if we do not engage them in these issues? We want them to be critical thinkers and to question the decisions of our government. If we are committed to developing civic competence among our young people, these kinds of learning activities are essential. Yet, because they are so politically charged and value-laden, the exploration of such topics requires that we educate teachers so that they can handle them confidently and successfully. This is one of the most challenging dimensions of social studies teacher preparation.

Rethinking the Traditional Social Studies Curriculum

Out of this particular experience with storyline, and my ongoing reflections about how best to prepare beginning teachers, has come my conviction that we must return to Brophy and Alleman's belief (1993) that what is critical to good social studies instruction is understanding the purposes of teaching. Social studies for civic competence requires a rethinking of the traditional social studies curriculum.

The standards movement has reinforced a traditional curriculum that in the past has been preoccupied with the acquisition of information as a primary outcome. To be sure, acquiring knowledge is important, but issues of depth versus coverage, application of knowledge, skill development, and civic efficacy are also essential to a successful social studies program. The NCSS standards have maintained

the status quo, as seems to be the case with the discipline-based standards of history, geography, and civics. Trends nationally and globally speak to issues that are affecting our young people in significant ways, and yet the social studies curriculum frequently gives these topics short shrift. The following section highlights areas of great importance.

Voices from the Inside (Poplin and Weeres 1992), a publication of The Institute for Education in Transformation, highlights schooling priorities through a study in which students, teachers, administrators, parents, and other school personnel participated in an intensive process of identifying the critical problems facing schools today. This inside view identified seven critical issues, five of which have direct implications for social studies education. The five critical issues are:

• *Relationships.* The most frequently identified issue was that of human relationships between teachers and students. Students placed a high priority on this factor and identified the importance of attributes such as caring, listening, understanding, respecting others, and being honest, open, and sensitive. Students of color reported that they frequently felt that teachers did not like or understand them.

Our preoccupation with the "what to learn" in the field has overshadowed the "how we learn." In teacher education programs, priorities frequently have been placed on curriculum and methods at the expense of developing the skills and dispositions that teachers need to work effectively on interpersonal relationships. These skills are important for adolescents, and particularly important for adolescents who need to learn about those whose cultural experiences are different from their own. If positive relationships—between teacher and students, as well as among students—do not exist in the classroom, social studies education for civic competence has little chance for success.

• *Race, culture, and class.* This theme was evident throughout the study and was the cause of much debate. While there was little consensus, students of color and some Euro-American students perceived schools to be racist and prejudiced. Students expressed interest about one another's culture but felt that schools failed to respond to that interest. Race, culture, and class are topics relevant to the social studies curriculum and intimately affect all students. Why are we not facilitating this understanding?

• *Values.* The data from the study suggested that there was wide agreement on the values related to education: honesty, integrity, beauty, care, justice, truth, courage, and meaningful hard work. "Students desire a network of adults (parents and teachers) with whom they can 'really talk about important things,' and want to have these conversations about values with one another" (14).

Once again, the social studies curriculum has given short shrift to values, with the mention of values education sending many social studies educators into hiding. The fact remains that our curriculum is value-laden, and in order to achieve the goal of civic competence, value discussions must take place. I suggest that the kinds of issues students refer to in this study are relevant to the social studies curriculum and important to helping students address the pressing social issues in which they are enmeshed.

Do we have the courage to meet this issue head on? Without taking some risks regarding the content of the curriculum, we can never achieve the goal of civic competence. My own experience of teaching about the reservation system in the storyline required that I create a learning experience that directly called into question the policies of the federal government. To address this issue meaningfully, students had to be personally in touch with the issue of the reservation system. That meant involving both their minds and their hearts in the issue, which meant my taking a responsible risk as an experienced educator. Beginning

teachers should be given that experience and guidance in order to feel confident and be effective in such important learning situations.

• *Teaching and learning.* The study reports that a frequent lament of students in the upper grades is that school is boring and has little relevance to their lives and future. "Teachers feel pressure to teach what is mandated and sometimes doubt its appropriateness for their students" (14). Consistently, students expressed "enthusiasm about learning experiences that are complex but understandable, full of rich meanings and discussions of values, require their own action, and those about which they have some choice" (15). This quotation is consistent with the learning principles outlined in "A Vision of Powerful Teaching and Learning in the Social Studies: Building Social Understanding and Civic Efficacy" (1993). We know how to achieve these goals, but do we have the will and perseverance to work toward achieving them?

The standards and testing movement may be the greatest obstacle to a schooling experience that responds to these needs. The movement creates the hidden curriculum that says curriculum content drives schooling rather than the needs of the students. A common banner is "Teacher as decision-maker," and yet the dominant message is "There are standards to be achieved and outcomes to be measured." This sends mixed messages to beginning teachers, whose common lament is "What am I supposed to teach?"

Teachers clearly need the flexibility to design a curriculum that is student centered, not mandated by a national committee of educators that is concerned about a political agenda. Broad educational goals can provide greater flexibility in creating a student-centered curriculum and yet maintain a pathway for teachers to follow in setting curriculum priorities. NCSS can play an important role in developing and supporting such a pathway.

• *Despair, hope, and the process of change.*

Hopelessness about schools was reflected by many of those participating in this study. "Paradoxically, hope seemed to emerge following honest dialogues about our collective despair. Participants are anxious for change and willing to participate in change they perceive as relevant" (16). Therein lies our opportunity to move toward the goal of civic competence as an outcome for the social studies curriculum.

Social studies education could make a significant contribution to the issues identified in this report. However, to do this we must actively seek to make fundamental changes not only in our day-to-day lessons with our beginning teachers but through our professional activities that set policy and standards within our universities, professional organizations, states, and nation.

Rethinking Teacher Preparation

As schooling has become increasingly complex, a new paradigm for teacher induction needs to be considered. I believe that most of us who are involved in the preparation of beginning teachers underestimate the difficulties these students face in trying to accomplish what we teach them. While university students generally rate their student teaching as the most valuable experience in their preparation for teaching, many of the goals of a teacher education program are not realized because of lack of cohesiveness between the student teaching setting and university program, time and curriculum constraints, teaching styles and personalities, and a myriad of other factors.

Teacher preparation programs must be better integrated, and social studies educators must work collaboratively with colleagues to create programs that place a high priority on the following:

• Providing solid grounding in subject matter. This should not take the form of cramming information into students' heads. Rather, beginning teachers must know more about their subjects so they can make well-reasoned decisions about curriculum priorities, matching the needs of students with curriculum goals that are important and meaningful and are not simply a march through a textbook or a series of historical events.

• Modeling an integrative curriculum. Both university professors and teachers need to collaborate more closely with professors and teachers in fields other than their own. Attention needs to be given to the natural connections among subject areas and to common curriculum goals. An overcrowded curriculum continues to place beginning teachers in an untenable situation, as each of the various professors is inclined to tout his or her field as most important. This process leaves the beginning teacher to sort through priorities and make sense of the various educational messages.

• Encouraging and aiding human growth and development. Developing meaningful relationships with students from a broad range of backgrounds must have special emphasis. In *A Sense of Belonging* (1993), five essential principles for effective education were outlined:

○A sense of self-esteem, both personal and cultural.

○A respect and tolerance for others, both as individuals and as members of ethnic/cultural groups.

○A sense of belonging, meaning that all must have a secure physical, emotional, and political focus within society.

○A sense of social responsibility, meaning an understanding that the diverse society in which we live must recognize the imperative to act with tolerance and responsibility in relation to social, political, cultural, and environmental factors.

○An appreciation of the importance of learning, meaning a recognition that knowledge, in whatever construction, is a means to new understandings, insights, creative opportunities, and an appreciation of the intercon-nectedness of our world. (13)

These principles must have center stage in social studies teacher preparation programs because they set the foundation for all else that follows.

• Increasing the emphasis on addressing values in the schooling process. We must build beginning teachers' confidence in addressing value-laden issues. Attacks by parents and special interest groups on schools and teachers who address value-laden issues receive a great deal of attention in the media. As a consequence, beginning teachers enter teacher preparation programs with high levels of anxiety about this topic. We must assist beginning teachers in dealing with value-laden issues by providing clearly articulated goals, solid grounding in the subject matter, appropriate strategies for learning about these topics, sensitivity to the particular environments touched by the controversy, and opportunities to teach these issues with support from university faculty. Strategies for working with parents and the community must be available, along with strategies for dealing with sensitive issues in particular communities. Understanding and commitment to democratic values and critical social issues facing our society and the world are important and vital to preparing students for civic competence.

• Making a commitment to civic competence the primary goal of social studies education. This move demands a refocusing of the social studies curriculum. An important priority is to provide opportunities for beginning teachers to explore the concept of civic competence and how it might be taught in today's classrooms. Previous learning experiences easily place the beginning teacher in a position to slip into old ways of teaching that probably do not place civic competence as a high priority. Curriculum planning that involves identifying civic competence outcomes, and strategies to

achieve those outcomes, must be an integral component of a social studies teacher preparation program.

• Creating a new induction paradigm. This action is essential to support innovative curriculum and teaching practices, as I realized in returning to teach in classrooms and using such strategies as storyline and cooperative learning. The principal teaching models that beginning teachers have are those from their own first sixteen years of education. If we desire to challenge those models and provide new models of teaching and organizing the curriculum, student teaching as we know it may be an outmoded model. Some attempts have been made to modify the experience; however, the traditional model dominates.

Changing this paradigm requires policy changes related to university programs, state certification, and current school practice. Clearly this goes beyond the field of social studies education. A paradigm shift that allows beginning teachers time to construct a curriculum within broad guidelines is a first step. In the rush to address the myriad of competencies, reflective thinking about curriculum priorities and the needs of learners is short-changed. Perhaps in a secondary setting, beginning teachers should teach one block of classes in order to allow thoughtful and reflective planning time, guided by university faculty and classroom teachers. If programs overload beginning teachers with large numbers of students and multiple content areas, the survival mode dominates and bad practices flourish. It may not be necessary to place student teachers in full-time teaching settings in order for them to be inducted into the profession.

Simply "borrowing" a teacher's classroom for a quarter or semester is not adequate. It is a situation that will never be repeated in that person's teaching career. The survivors of traditional student teaching experiences lament the preoccupation with "fitting in" with a classroom teacher's methods and curriculum, which are frequently in direct conflict with the teacher education program and meeting the university supervisor's agenda. In a new kind of apprentice program, the "student teacher" might be under contract with a school district on a part-time basis. In such a program, the student teacher owns the teaching situation and has time for significant planning for instruction. Additionally, expert support from the university and school district would be essential to developing the knowledge, skills, and dispositions necessary for a beginning teacher. While this new approach might not offer all the solutions to preparing beginning teachers, it does provide ways to move student teachers beyond a survivalist mode to a reflective mode accompanied by adequate instructional support for new strategies and curricular innovations.

Conclusion

The conditions affecting today's classrooms make our challenge as teachers even more arduous than in the past. We must be willing to take uncompromising stands on the importance of civic competence as a schooling priority. We must listen to "the voices from inside" that are clearly aware of the problems of schools. We must have the political will to make our voices heard among the policymakers, parents, media, and special interest groups. Educators in charge of teacher preparation must work to change their paradigms in order to prepare new teachers for today's issues and classrooms.

The National Council for the Social Studies must make its collective voice heard. We must all work for powerful social studies teaching that will enable young people to develop the ability to make informed and reasoned decisions for the public good as citizens of a culturally diverse, democratic society in an interdependent world.

References

Brophy, J. E., and J. Alleman. "Elementary Social Studies Should Be Driven by Major Social Education Goals." *Social Education* 57, no. 1 (1993): 27-32.

CIDREE/UNESCO. *A Sense of Belonging.* Paris: Section for Humanistic, Cultural & International Education, UNESCO, 1993.

McGuire, M. E., and K. Schlick Noe. "The Early People of the Pacific Northwest Coast." Unpublished curriculum unit, 1994.

National Commission on Excellence in Education. *A Nation at Risk: The Imperative for Educational Reform.* Washington, D.C.: U.S. Government Printing Office, 1983.

National Council for the Social Studies. "A Vision of Powerful Teaching and Learning in the Social Studies: Building Social Understanding for Civic Efficacy." *Social Education* 57, no. 5 (1993): 213-23.

Poplin, M., and J. Weeres. *Voices from the Inside.* Claremont, Calif.: The Institute for Education in Transformation at the Claremont Graduate School, 1992.

Shaver, J. P., ed. *Handbook of Research on Social Studies Teaching and Learning.* New York: Macmillan Publishing Company, 1991.

NCSS *and Research*

Jack R. Fraenkel
San Francisco State University

SOCIAL STUDIES RESEARCH DID NOT REALLY BEGIN TO COME INTO its own until the early 1960s. This new attention to research was largely an outgrowth of three interrelated factors:

1. An increase in the number of reviews of social studies research conducted by scholars, many of whom were members of the National Council for the Social Studies (e.g., Gross and Badger 1960; Harrison and Solomon 1964; Skettering and Sundeen 1969);

2. The numerous calls that began at that time (some from NCSS members) to reform the teaching of the social studies in elementary and secondary schools,[1] and the accompanying formation of committees, commissions and projects by various social science associations (e.g., the American Historical Association, the American Anthropological Association, the American Sociological Association, etc.) to develop ideas and prepare curricular materials to bring about such reform; and

3. The formation of the College and University Faculty Assembly (CUFA) at the 1963 NCSS Annual Meeting.

As its name implies, CUFA initially was comprised of college and university faculty members who had an interest in social studies education; these were usually professors who taught social studies methods. Over time, the membership of CUFA has expanded to include other social studies professionals, such as student teaching supervisors, school district curriculum developers, publishers' representatives, and state social studies specialists. For the most part, however, college and university faculty remain the backbone of the organization.

With the formation of CUFA, NCSS recognized, at least to some degree, the important role of research in furthering the goals of social studies education. Here is what one of CUFA's founding members had to say at the time:

> This is a real step forward for the college and university people who are members of NCSS. Having a separate part of NCSS devoted exclusively to the concerns of college people is something we've needed for a long time. It will enable those of us who have strong theoretical and research interests to get together on a more formal basis at the annual meetings each year. I think it can't help but benefit all of us who are interested in pursuing our research interests on a more systematic basis than we've been able to do so far.

NCSS immediately included CUFA as a part of the larger body and agreed to provide space at the annual meetings for CUFA members to report on their research and scholarship. The formation of CUFA led, in November 1973, to the creation of a peer review research journal, *Theory and Research in Social Education* (TRSE).

In October 1963, before the NCSS annual meeting, in recognition of a general belief that the social studies curriculum in the nation's classrooms was in need of major revision, the Maxwell Graduate School of Citizenship and Public Affairs and the School of Education at Syracuse University sponsored a conference entitled "Needed Research in the Teaching of the Social Studies," under the auspices of the Cooperative Research Branch of the United States Office of Education. It was jointly sponsored by the National Council for the Social Studies and the United States Office of Education. This event, so far as I can tell, was the first organized effort to overcome the lag between what was supposedly known from social science research and what was taught in the schools, to identify needed areas of research, and to stimulate research in critical areas (Price 1963).

Since then, a sizable number of studies have been conducted (for the most recent reviews, see Shaver 1991; Thornton 1994). The authors of much of this research have been NCSS members. Individual studies continue to be done each year by a handful of researchers (again, mostly by NCSS members). Other journals in which NCSS members publish their research include the *Journal of Social Studies Research* (JSSR), the *Social Studies*, the *Review of Educational Research*, the *Elementary School Journal*, the *Journal of Geography*, and the research section of *Social Education* (SE). Admittedly, not very much research is to be found in these journals. Unpublished reports of research also appear from time to time in *Resources in Education* (RIE), published monthly by the ERIC Clearinghouse on Social Studies Education at Indiana University.

Although a fair amount of social studies research has been and continues to be undertaken each year, none of it has been either directed or sponsored by NCSS. The national council did, however, sponsor the production and publication of a number of research bulletins during the 1970s and 1980s (e.g., see Atwood 1986) and more recently, the *Handbook of Research on Social Studies Teaching And Learning* (Shaver 1991). A number of reviews of social studies research have appeared over the years (e.g., see Angell 1991; Metcalf 1963; Shaver 1991; Thornton 1994), as well as reviews of the social science disciplines whose subject matter makes up much (some would say most) of the social studies curriculum (e.g., see Carroll et al. 1979; Rice and Cobb 1978; Torney et al 1975). However, only those that have appeared as chapters in NCSS bulletins dealing with research (e.g., see Hunkins et al. 1977; Stanley 1985) have been sponsored directly by NCSS, although most of the authors have been NCSS members.

The largest amount of research done in social studies education continues to be that found in the doctoral dissertations.[2] Abstracts of these appear in *Dissertation Abstracts International*. Reviews of dissertation research in social studies have been compiled by several scholars, most of whom have been NCSS members (e.g., see Chapin 1974; Hepburn and Dahler 1985; McPhie 1964), although the organization did not sponsor their efforts. Most of the research work in the field of social studies continues to be done by individual researchers, with little, if any, of it supported or endorsed by the professional association of social studies teachers.

Changes in the Nature of Social Studies Research

Most research in social studies education in the past has been quantitative in nature. For example, Fraenkel and Wallen (1991), reviewing 183 empirical studies published in TRSE, JSSR and SE during the ten years from 1979 to 1988, found that 85 percent were experiments, quasi-experiments, correlations, or surveys. Fourteen percent involved some type of qualitative study. Similarly, Saxe et al. (in preparation), in a review of social studies doctoral dissertations, found that 63 percent of the dissertations completed during the years 1982-1991 were quantitative studies. Qualitative studies do appear to be increasing in number, however (Preissle-Goetz and LeCompte 1991). Saxe and his colleagues, for example, found a considerable increase in qualitative dissertations[3] (30 percent of the total as compared to 9 percent of the total for the period 1977-1982), and the number of qualitative studies being submitted to TRSE has increased considerably in the last few years. Whether or not this trend will continue remains to be seen.

Weaknesses in Social Studies Research

Many critics have described much of the research produced by social studies investiga-

tors as flawed in both conception and design. The vast majority of the studies reported are one-time efforts, conducted by individual researchers, with no subsequent attempt to replicate the work, conduct related studies, or develop a consistent and continuous line of inquiry. Few topics are followed up over time or dealt with in depth. Furthermore, there are few organized centers of scholars engaged in ongoing research in social studies education at the current time. In addition, the number of doctorates in social studies education has been declining in recent years.[4]

Both quantitative and qualitative studies conducted by social studies researchers have been criticized as lacking in several respects:

• Frequent criticisms of quantitative studies are: failure to investigate significant questions; inadequate descriptions of samples; vague definitions of variables; vague definitions of treatments; brief or weak administration of treatments; failure to apply reliability and validity checks; failure to check on threats to internal validity; inappropriate or incorrect use of statistical inference tests; lack of determination of durability of results; failure to replicate studies; too many individual studies in different settings, with different samples or under different conditions; overgeneralization of findings (see Fraenkel and Wallen 1991).

• Frequent criticisms of qualitative studies are: provision of too much insignificant detail; failure to tie-in to larger or more significant questions; failure to explain the significance of observations for understanding the human condition; frequent lack of definition of a meaningful unit of analysis; failure to distinguish isolated events from underlying cultural patterns; tendency by authors to overgeneralize findings; insufficient allotment of time for the collection of data; lack of full-time participant observation; lack of continuous observation; overreliance on classroom observations as the unit of analysis (see Palonsky 1987).

Although the quality of much social studies

research remains a concern, a number of well-done individual studies have recently appeared. A few examples are ethnographies (e.g., Bickmore 1993), comparative experiments (e.g., Avery et al. 1992), summative reviews (e.g., Harwood 1992); content analyses (e.g., Wade 1993), and observations of social studies classrooms in which teachers emphasized higher-order thinking (e.g., Newmann 1991).

Nevertheless, it must be admitted that the quality of social studies research has not been a central concern of NCSS. Although there have been a few outcries by individual members from time to time (e.g., see Fraenkel 1987; Shaver and Larkins 1973), and an occasional session at one or two of the annual meetings has been directed toward this end, NCSS has never appointed a formal committee to investigate this matter, nor is there any mechanism currently in place to assist members who desire to improve their research capabilities.

The Role of the Council

What, then, has been the role of NCSS with regard to research in social studies? Sad to say, NCSS has never had a formal policy regarding research. The term "research" is defined only briefly in the NCSS policy manual:

> *Research is defined as systematic scholarly inquiry into questions of significance. Research is a fundamental part of social studies and provides reliable knowledge for effective practice in social studies.* (84)

Although the definition refers to research as "a fundamental part of social studies," the council has never produced a set of "research standards" similar to those for the preparation of social studies teachers (NCSS 1992).

NCSS's major activities with regard to research have been the following: (a) establishment of a Committee on Research, which

meets every year at the annual meeting; (b) provision of space at the annual meetings, where CUFA members and others interested in research may present papers and make presentations; (c) sponsorship and publication of bulletins dealing with research topics; (d) publication of reviews and reports of research in *Social Education*; (e) support for *Theory and Research in Social Education*; and (f) sponsorship of the *Handbook of Research on Social Studies Teaching and Learning*.

The NCSS Committee on Research

The research committee of NCSS is an advisory (as opposed to an operations) committee that meets annually at the national meeting in November of each year. It is made up of twenty-five NCSS members, who serve for a three-year term, plus one member who is a liaison from the Board of Directors. Members are appointed each year by the president from a list made up of volunteers provided by the national office, members who ask the president personally to serve, or those whom the president has asked to serve.

All NCSS advisory committees are charged with a number of purposes and duties. Those that are particularly applicable to the research committee are stated in the policy manual as follows:

- To identify current research being conducted as well as new research findings.
- To propose courses of action for NCSS to the NCSS Board of Directors, based on trends, issues, laws and research.
- To propose methods and audiences for disseminating information about trends, research, promising practices, issues or problems to the Board of Directors. (45-6)

The committee does not, however, sponsor or conduct any research directly. In the main, members are left to pursue their own inclinations and interests regarding research projects they perceive to be important.

The membership of the committee is made up of a variety of types, including classroom teachers, college and university professors, and curriculum specialists. Attendance at the yearly meetings is generally good, with usually about twelve members out of a twenty-five-person committee present. The committee's focus is highly dependent on the energy and interests of the current chairperson (who is elected for only a one-year term). Many of the high school members are unable to get support from their districts to attend.

What value, then, does the committee have? Four services are provided by the committee. First, three subcommittees are appointed to seek nominations for three research awards that are presented at the annual meeting. These are the NCSS Research Award in Social Studies Education (for the best individual piece of social studies research each year); the Outstanding Dissertation Award (for the best Ph.D. or Ed.D. social studies dissertation each year); and the Career Research Award (for an outstanding lifetime career conducting social studies research). Members of these subcommittees seek nominations, gather supporting materials, evaluate nominees' contributions, and determine the award winner. Service on one of these subcommittees takes a considerable amount of time and is the major activity in which members of the whole committee participate. As with all NCSS committees, all of the members are volunteers.

A second value of the committee is that it serves as a forum where possible research topics of interest to the organization as a whole can surface, be discussed and, on occasion, brought to the attention of the council's Board of Directors for verbal support, endorsement, or action. Third, the committee can, as it has on at least one occasion, serve as a vehicle to produce a publication directed toward making research more understandable and palatable for members of the organization as a whole

(e.g., see Cornbleth 1986). And fourth, the committee offers a place where members can get together to discuss research and pursue topics and ideas of interest.

Here is what a former committee chair had to say about the committee's value:

We get a pretty fair turnout at our meetings each year. The meetings are very valuable to those who come. These are the people who will do what needs to be done. We get to kick ideas around and, on more than one occasion, we have suggested things to the officers of NCSS and to the Board of Directors that they ought to consider. But also, the Committee provides a voice for those who are interested in research where they can have a say. And at least it keeps the officers of the Council aware that they should be thinking about research, even if (formally) they often do not.

Here is what another chair had to say:

You need a critical mass. The problem is that, other than the awards subcommittees, the committee-as-a-whole is largely inactive during the rest of the year. We just don't have any way to follow up on research, to pursue a line of inquiry. The Council should do this, but it doesn't.

The Annual Meetings

There is no question that NCSS provides a valuable service to those interested in research by providing opportunities at the annual meetings for members to present papers on research topics of interest, as well as reports of actual research they have conducted, are currently conducting, or plan to conduct in the future. Although most of these sessions are held during the CUFA sessions, some appear during the general NCSS schedule. Most of the research in social studies education is done by university professors—primarily because, unlike classroom teachers, they have the time to do it. It is not uncommon, however, to see some reports of research presented during the latter parts of each annual meeting, when most of the classroom teachers are in attendance. Occasionally, reports of joint university/teacher research are presented and, in a particularly welcome development, reports are made by classroom teachers themselves of ongoing classroom research (often referred to as "action research").

Something else occurs at the annual meetings that is conducive to research: the informal conversations that go on in the halls after sessions, at lunch or dinner, over coffee or tea, and/or at the social events. Here members search out and find friends and colleagues and find out what they are doing, hear reports of as-yet-unpublished work in progress, and, in general, catch up on "what's happening" with others in the social studies research community. This is extremely valuable to everyone involved and is, in fact, why many members attend the annual meeting.

This is what one member said about the value of these informal conversations:

I wouldn't miss an annual meeting, but not for the reasons you might suspect. I am interested, of course, in the formal papers and reports that are presented and what I hear in the sessions, but I find the most value in the conversations I have at breakfast and in the halls with colleagues I respect about what they are doing—this gives me some ideas I would not find in the journals. Sort of information on the cutting edge, you might say.

The Research Bulletins

NCSS has also sponsored, over the years, the design, development, and production of a number of bulletins dealing with various research topics (e.g., research on critical thinking). Under the direction of the Publications Committee, an editor is selected who, in turn, asks a number of members (usually, but not exclusively, CUFA members) to write a chapter on some aspect of research. Examples of past chapters include: research on social studies learning and instruction with regard to values (Ehman 1977); research on the diffusion of social studies innovations (Hahn 1977); a review of ethnographic research studies as they inform issues of social studies curriculum and instruction (White 1985); and recent research in the foundations of social education (Stanley 1985a). The content of these chapters includes a review and synthesis of the literature on the topic, usually followed by some analysis and commentary by the author.

Once a first draft of a chapter is prepared, the manuscript is reviewed by members of the social studies community, usually university professors or other scholars who are knowledgeable about the topic. The reviewers are chosen by the Publications Committee and/or the chairperson of the social studies research special interest group of the American Educational Research Association. In addition, reviewers are often appointed by various other NCSS committees (e.g., the Committee on Sexism and Social Justice) to help the authors avoid bias in their research presentations .

The writing of these chapters, although beneficial to both the author and the social studies community, requires a tremendous amount of time and effort. The production and distribution of these bulletins to the membership are tremendous services to all who wish to keep current on the status of research on social studies topics. One such author, a CUFA member, said the following about this work:

There's no question that these chapters take time. They surely do. But it is work that needs to be done if we are to keep current about what research is being done in social studies education. Actually, I enjoy it, because it allows me to get into the literature and see what has been happening, and it also allows me to bring myself and interested others up to date.

Here is what another CUFA member had to say:

The research bulletins are one of the most beneficial things we get from belonging to NCSS. They are, to put it simply, invaluable to my development as a professional.

These bulletins are provided free to comprehensive members of the organization and made available at a reduced cost to all other members.

Reviews and Reports of Research in Social Education

From time to time, reviews and reports of research are also published in a special section of *Social Education*. These articles differ from those published in *Theory and Research in Social Education* in that they present research that is of special interest to (and on occasion has been conducted by) classroom teachers rather than university professors. James Shaver, a former NCSS president and the first editor of the research section, describes how the creation of this feature came about:

I had submitted an article to Dan Roselle, who at the time was the editor of Social Education. *Dan said that he did not want to publish the piece in the journal, since it was not directed toward the classroom teacher and he (Roselle) felt that should be the focus of the articles in* Social Education. *I then suggested to Dan that it might be a good idea to publish research articles of interest to classroom teachers. "Why not," I said, "have a special section of research specifically containing reports of such studies?" Dan, after thinking it over, agreed. That is how the special research section came into being.*

Theory and Research in Social Education

Perhaps the council's most significant support is that provided the editor of *Theory and Research in Social Education*, the journal of the College and University Faculty Assembly (CUFA) of NCSS. Although TRSE is edited and produced at a university, the council prepares the mailing list of recipients and covers all mailing expenses.

After the founding of TRSE in 1973 and a somewhat shaky start (only one issue was published each year for its first three years), the journal is now recognized as the premier research journal in the field of social studies education. Four issues are published each year, with each issue containing anywhere from three to five articles. There are no limitations on the length of manuscripts that may be submitted.

About forty articles are submitted each year, and approximately 15 percent are accepted for publication. In addition, books of interest to social studies educators are reviewed, letters to the editor are published, and a lively exchange of views on various topics is presented from time to time.

Decisions on the kinds of article published in the journal are guided by the following mission statement:

Theory and Research in Social Education is designed to stimulate and communicate systematic research and thinking in social education. Its purpose is to foster the creation and exchange of ideas and research findings that will expand knowledge about purposes, conditions, and effects of schooling and education about society and social relations.

Here is what one university professor, a regular subscriber, had to say in a letter to the editor:

I want to tell you how much I enjoy TRSE. I look forward to its arrival every few months.

It keeps me current about what is going on in the field. I also feel that the research articles, studies, and positions that are presented are of equal quality to other disciplinary areas, and that we in social studies education can be proud of our research efforts.

The Handbook of Research on Social Studies Teaching and Learning.

In 1987, the Publications Committee invited Jim Shaver, a former NCSS President, to serve as editor of a massive and authoritative handbook on research that was then in its formative stages. Shaver, a professor at Utah State University, was interested in research, had been editor of the research section in *Social Education*, and had himself conducted research on a number of social studies topics. After some consideration, Shaver agreed to take on the challenge. The Publications Committee had nominated an editorial advisory board, consisting of some six members of NCSS, for Shaver's review and approval. Shaver and the board met in Washington, D.C., in January 1988 to formulate a plan for the handbook and to develop a list of possible authors of chapters. Shaver than returned to Utah State to begin the somewhat arduous task of contacting potential authors by telephone and letter. Although not all scholars contacted committed to writing or reviewing a chapter, most did. The result was the publication, in fall 1991, of the *Handbook of Research on Social Studies Teaching and Learning.*

The Handbook is more than 650 pages, divided into 53 chapters, presenting reviews of research dealing with almost every imaginable aspect of social studies education. Most of the chapters were written by NCSS members. The Handbook truly is a major contribution to the documentation, organization, and analysis of social studies research.

What role did NCSS play in the development of the Handbook? Here is what Shaver had to say:

The Editorial Advisory Board provided me with essential assistance in conceptualizing the Handbook, suggesting authors, reacting to manuscripts, and providing me with other advice when I requested it during the course of the project. It was, nevertheless, their moral support that I appreciated most. (Shaver 1991, xi)

Conclusion

Although NCSS does not have a formal policy on research, it has supported research in a number of ways. Perhaps it is doing more than can be expected. Perhaps it is doing all it can, given the nature of the organization. Still, we can hope that it will do more and that, at the very least, it will develop a set of standards for research as it has done for so many other areas.

Notes

[1] These cries were reflected in a volume published by the American Council of Learned Societies and the National Council for the Social Studies that contained a number of chapters on the relationship between several of the social science disciplines and the social studies (ACLS 1962).

[2] Saxe, Jackson, and Mraz (in preparation) located 499 social studies dissertations in the ten-year span, 1982-1991.

[3] As used here, the term "qualitative" refers to both historical and ethnographic studies.

[4] From an average of 100 dissertations completed per year between the years 1969-1973 to an average of 49.9 for the years 1982-1991 (Saxe, Jackson, and Mraz, in preparation).

References

American Council of Learned Societies and the National Council for the Social Studies.

The Social Studies and the Social Sciences. New York: Harcourt, Brace and World, 1962.

Angell, A. V. "Democratic Climates in Elementary School Classrooms: A Review of Theory and Research." *Theory and Research in Social Education* 19, no. 3 (1991): 241-67.

Atwood, V. E., ed. *Elementary School Social Studies: Research as a Guide to Practice.* Bulletin 79. Washington, D.C.: National Council for the Social Studies, 1986.

Avery, P. G., K. Bird, S. Johnstone, J. L. Sullivan, and K. Thalhammer. "Exploring Political Tolerance with Adolescents." *Theory and Research in Social Education* 20, no. 4 (1992): 386-420.

Bickmore, K. "Learning Inclusion/Inclusion in Learning: Citizenship Education for a Pluralistic Society." *Theory and Research in Social Education* 21, no. 4 (1993): 341-84.

Carroll, W. E., A. Jones, L. Gelfand, W. C. Heywood, R. Fitch, P. Kinter, and E. Hawley. *The Teaching of History in the Public High Schools of Iowa.* Grinnell, Iowa: Grinnell College, 1979.

Chapin, J. R. *Social Studies Dissertations: 1969-1973.* Boulder, Colo.: ERIC Clearinghouse for Social Studies Education, 1974.

Cornbleth, C., ed. *An Invitation to Research in Social Education.* Bulletin 77. Washington, D.C.: National Council for the Social Studies, 1986.

Ehman, L. H. "Research on Social Studies Curriculum and Instruction: Values." In *Review of Research in Social Studies Education: 1970-1975,* edited by F. P. Hunkins, 55-96. Washington, D.C.: National Council for the Social Studies; Boulder, Colo.: Social Science Education Consortium, 1977.

Fraenkel, J. R. "Toward Improving Research in Social Studies Education." *Theory and Research in Social Education* 25, no. 3 (1987): 203-22.

Fraenkel, J. R., and N. E. Wallen. "Quantitative Research in Social Studies Education." In *Handbook of Research on Social Studies Teaching and Learning,* edited by J. P. Shaver. New York: Macmillan, 1991: 67-82.

Gross, R. E., and W. V. Badger. "Social Studies." In *Encyclopedia of Educational Research,* 3d ed., edited by C. W. Harris. New York: Macmillan, 1960.

Hahn, Carole L. "Research on the Diffusion of Social Studies Innovations." In *Review of Research in Social Studies Education: 1970-1975,* edited by F. P. Hunkins, 137-78. Washington, D.C.: National Council for the Social Studies; Boulder, Colo.: Social Science Education Consortium, 1977.

Harrison, S. W., and R. J. Solomon. "Review of Research in the Teaching of Social Studies: 1964." *Social Education* 28 (1964): 277-92.

Harwood, A. M. "Classroom Climate and Civic Education in Secondary Social Studies Research: Antecedents and Findings." *Theory and Research in Social Education* 20, no. 1 (1992): 447-86.

Hepburn, M. A., and A. Dahler. "An Overview of Social Studies Dissertations, 1977-1982." *Theory and Research in Social Education* 13, no. 2 (1985): 78-82.

Hunkins, F. P., L. H. Ehman, C. L. Hahn, P. H. Martorella, and J. L. Tucker. *Review of Reseach in Social Studies Education: 1970-1975.* Washington, D.C.: National Council for the Social Studies; Boulder, Colo.: ERIC Clearinghouse for Social Studies/Social Science Education and the Social Science Education Consortium, 1977.

McPhie, W. E. *Dissertations in Social Studies Education: A Comprehensive Guide.* Research Bulletin 2. Washington, D.C.: National Council for the Social Studies, 1964.

Metcalf, Lawrence. "Research on Teaching the Social Studies." In *Handbook of Research on Teaching,* edited by N. L. Gage. Chicago: Rand McNally & Co., 1963.

National Council for the Social Studies. "Standards for the Preparation of Social Studies Teachers." *Social Education* 56, no. 5 (1992): 271-73.

National Council for the Social Studies. *Policy Manual.* Washington, D.C.: National Council for the Social Studies, n.d.

Newmann, F. M. "Classroom Thoughtfulness and Students' Higher Order Thinking: Common Indicators and Diverse Social Studies Courses."

Theory and Research in Social Education 19, no. 4 (1991): 410-33.

Palonsky, S. B. "Ethnographic Scholarship and Social Education." *Theory and Research in Social Education* 15, no. 1 (1987): 77-87.

Preissle-Goetz, J. and M. D. LeCompte. "Qualitative Research in Social Studies Education." In *Handbook of Research on Social Studies Teaching and Learning*, edited by J. P. Shaver. New York: Macmillan, 1991: 56-66.

Price, Roy A. *Needed Research in the Teaching of the Social Studies*. Research Bulletin 1. Washington, D.C.: National Council for the Social Studies, 1963.

Rice, M. J., and R. L. Cobb. *What Can Children Learn in Geography? A Review of the Research*. Boulder, Colo.: ERIC Clearinghouse for Social Science/Social Studies Education, 1978.

Saxe, D. W., M. L. Jackson, and M. Mraz. "Dissertation Research in Social Studies: 1982-1991" (manuscript in preparation).

Shaver, J. P., ed. *Handbook of Research on Social Studies Teaching and Learning*. New York: Macmillan, 1991.

Shaver, J. P., and A. G. Larkins. "Research on Teaching Social Studies." In *Second Handbook of Research on Teaching*, edited by R. M. W. Travers. Chicago: Rand McNally, 1973.

Skettering, J. R., and J. E. Sundeen. "Social Studies Education." In *Encyclopedia of Educational Research*, 4th ed., edited by R. L. Ebel. New York: Macmillan, 1969.

Stanley, W. B. "Recent Research in the Foundations of Social Education: 1976-1983." In *Review of Research in Social Studies Education: 1976-1983*, edited by W. B. Stanley. Washington, D.C.: National Council for the Social Studies; Boulder, Colo.: ERIC Clearinghouse for Social Studies/Social Science Education and the Social Science Education Consortium, 1985 [1985a].

Stanley, W. B., ed. *Review of Research in Social Studies Education: 1976-1983*. Washington, D.C.: National Council for the Social Studies; Boulder, Colo.: ERIC Clearinghouse for Social Studies/Social Science Education and the Social Science Education Consortium, 1985 [1985b].

Thornton, S. J. "The Social Studies Near Century's End: Reconsidering Patterns of Curriculum and Instruction." In *Review of Research in Education* (20), edited by L. Darling-Hammond. Washington, D.C.: American Educational Research Association, 1994.

Torney, J., A. N. Oppenheim and R. F. Farnen. *Civic Education in Ten Countries: An Empirical Study*. New York: John Wiley, 1975.

Wade, R. C. "Content Analysis of Social Studies Textbooks: A Review of Ten Years of Research." *Theory and Research in Social Education* 21, no. 3 (1993): 232-56.

White, J. J. "What Works for Teachers: A Review of Ethnographic Research Studies as They Inform Issues on Social Studies Curriculum and Instruction." In *Review of Research in Social Studies Education: 1976-1983*, edited by W. B. Stanley, 215-308. Washington, D.C.: National Council for the Social Studies; Boulder, Colo.: Social Science Education Consortium, 1985.

NCSS *and Social Crises*

Jack L. Nelson
Rutgers University
and
William R. Fernekes
Hunterdon Central High School

A CRISIS IS OFTEN IN THE EYE OF THE BEHOLDER AND SUBJECT TO argument, but crises ebb and flow through individual and group life. Social crises are recognized by their scale and impact, by their extensiveness and severity in disrupting normal life. The plague and war are obvious examples, but social upheavals also can be structural or psychological. Major economic disorders, basic challenges to societal values, and high level political disarray are examples. Social crises are important and controversial, stimulating intensified and highly emotional debate, scapegoating, and excessive responses. These effects threaten the foundations of democracy, reasoned discourse, and sound education. Social crises are thus of significant concern for social studies education.

Social Studies, NCSS, and Crisis Study

Social studies is the teaching field most connected to the study of social crises. It is a necessary linkage, whether through the perspectives of archaeology, ancient history, politics, geography, ideology, current issues, or future studies. It is also a linkage understood in the profession. In 1921 in a hotel room in Atlantic City, a safe distance from war and plague, the National Council for the Social Studies (NCSS) was established under its original title, The National Council of Teachers of the Social Studies. NCSS was founded to provide leadership in social studies teaching and in the examination of issues; a 1923 amendment to the NCSS constitution specified the investigation of social problems.

The complex and controversial nature of social crises demands more than the simplistic and unattainable notion that we can avoid repeating errors of the past by mere historical study. NCSS defines social studies as an integrated field, drawing upon a wide variety of subjects and requiring intellectual freedom for teachers and students. The proper study of controversial social crises is well within the role of NCSS, which advocates social education about historical and contemporary crises. This advocacy is based on the need, in a democratic society, for enlightened understanding of issues and the development of critical thinking for more sophisticated civic participation and social improvement. NCSS, in its claim to leadership, thus has a fundamental interest in social crises.

Fulfilling the claim to leadership in this work, however, requires more than mere interest. It also requires organizational recognition of social crises and thoughtful development and expression of influential views on their educational aspects. NCSS's record in pursuit of this leadership appears in official documents, formal resolutions, publications, and known actions.

To gather information for this chapter, we examined the NCSS archives at Teachers College, Columbia University, and pertinent publications. During the early years of NCSS, the key journal was *The Historical Outlook*, founded in 1909 as a journal of the American Historical Association (AHA) under the name *The History Teacher's Magazine*. After the founding of NCSS, *The Historical Outlook* published NCSS yearbooks as its December issues in 1922, 1923, and 1924. *The Historical Outlook* changed its name to *The Social Studies* in 1934, and that journal became the official NCSS journal in 1935. *Social Education* was established by NCSS in 1937, and has remained its major publication. We read issues of each of these journals to supplement our review of the archives.

We do not claim that this chapter is exhaustive in its study of social crises or the records of NCSS; indeed, it may lack insights to be gained from unexamined sources. However, it represents our interpretation of the reaction of NCSS to selected social crises over the past seventy-five years. Specific crises we selected for examination are the Depression, World War II, elements of the civil rights movement, the McCarthy period, and the Vietnam War. We start with a very brief social context for the early days of NCSS.

The Early Days Surrounding NCSS

NCSS emerged between twentieth-century social crises of war and depression. World War I, following fifty years of tinder box politics among the nations of Europe, was ignited by the killing of the Austrian Archduke Franz Ferdinand in Sarajevo in 1914. (Tragically, Sarajevo returned to public consciousness in the 1990s as a symbol of massive violence and ethnic fervor, as though little was learned by the mere study of history.) Although NCSS was not yet established in 1914, many social subjects educators taught about the war and its aftermath, even though the United States had tried to avoid active participation and had, in fact, stayed out of most of it (*The War Issues Course* 1918; Barnard 1918).

By the time NCSS was formed, World War I had ceased. The war ended, however, under a faulty treaty and a fatally weak League of Nations initiated without approval of the United States Senate. The façade of peace was a popular image, hiding the emergence of other global and societal crises. Persistent strands of xenophobia appeared in the United States in the 1920s, including the following:
- a "red scare" about Communist infiltration into American life and schools;
- questionable convictions and executions of Sacco and Vanzetti as anti-American examples of atheists and anarchists;
- anti-semitic and racist nationalism exemplified by increasingly public and violent activities of the Ku Klux Klan against blacks and sympathetic whites;

- anti-unionism based on fear of Communist infiltration, and
- the first Congressional mandates for immigration quotas in response to nativist fears that "American" stock was being diluted and funds wasted providing education and welfare for foreigners.

In addition to war weariness and nationalistic fears, conflicting strains of human frailty and exuberance from post-war economic growth were evident in American popular culture: the Charleston, flappers, flamboyant dress, fantasy pre-talkie movies and radio, the Scopes trial, and literary works by Sinclair Lewis, Eugene O'Neill, Edna St. Vincent Millay, John Dos Passos, F. Scott Fitzgerald, Ernest Hemingway, and Lewis Mumford. Tensions between puritanical restrictiveness and democratic liberalism were reflected in constitutional legislation on two significant reform movements of the period: prohibiting the consumption of alcohol and extending the vote to women. This was a propitious time to initiate NCSS as a voice for the profession in examination of social issues and academic freedom; it was also a period of lull before the onset of the worldwide depression.

The Depression and NCSS

For today's older Americans, two moments define the twentieth century: the Depression and World War II. The Depression imposed severe restrictions on masses of people, caused the dislocation of many, and led to a widespread critique of the government and economic structures by all but the relatively untouched wealthy. It seriously threatened the stability of individuals, families, and the nation. For employed teachers, the decade from 1929 to 1939 was difficult, but not as destructive as it was for the unemployed. Social studies teachers taught about current events, economics, sociology, history, human

suffering, world affairs and government programs in that period. Some encouraged critical examination of issues and various courses of action to improve the society. Some taught self-reliant moralism and slogans under the guise of character education. Some taught nationalistic pride and fear of communists, anarchists, and New Dealers. Some taught revolutionary ideas to reconstruct society and schooling. And some were baffled or restrained by controversy: they taught the standard archival history courses, ignoring the Depression and other social issues.

NCSS provided no apparent early leadership to the field on the topic of the Depression. Bowers (1969), in a historical study of progressive educators in the Depression, cited the American Historical Association (AHA) for reinforcing progressive social reconstructionists but did not mention any work of NCSS. There is little in NCSS literature from 1929 to 1932 on the Depression. In *The Historical Outlook* in 1932, a high school principal addressed the NEA section on social sciences, recommending progressive books and magazines for social studies instruction to interpret the economic situation of the day, while arguing that social studies should integrate the separate disciplines to teach about issues better (Morrissett, 1932). *The Historical Outlook* also carried a statement on the Depression and the Schools from an NEA Joint Commission on the Emergency in Education (1933), but it addressed the loss of funds for education exclusively, and was not directed to teaching or curriculum. By 1939, NCSS had a committee on the "Use of WPA Materials," but that effort hardly represents leadership (NCSS 1939-40). Depressingly, we must conclude that NCSS offered little leadership in study of the Depression.

World War II and the NCSS

The looming international crisis of World

War II was of more apparent interest to NCSS. In 1933, *The Historical Outlook* featured an article examining the stake that the United States had in the Sino-Japanese dispute (Sherwood 1933). The same issue carried startling information on new Nazi German school requirements to teach nationalistic history to reinstill "German heroism" in the minds of youth and to preach against the "un-German" (Enderis 1933).

As 1939 approached, NCSS gave teachers signals and ideas about the worsening international situation and the need for social studies education on such topics. More importantly, some NCSS leaders recognized how xenophobia can make the study of crises highly controversial and how good social education requires teacher and student freedoms. Consequently, the 1937 NCSS Yearbook focused on propaganda education, in response to nationalistic zeal around the world. The NCSS annual meeting of 1938, in Pittsburgh, heard speakers stress the need to consider issues such as "international law and peace" (Notes and News 1939). Although some authors tried to focus on teaching peace (Winter 1939), NCSS publications carried many notices to teachers about the threat of war. Teachers were informed of Foreign Policy Association pamphlets on "The Nazi Drive to the East" and "International Aid to German Refugees" (Notes and News 1939). The "Have You Read?" column in *Social Education* noted current articles on the crisis in Europe, war in China, and unrest in Japan (Crane 1939).

Later issues in 1939 featured articles on Nazi propaganda in Czechoslovakia (Clough 1939), and a long bibliographic essay by a political scientist examining *Mein Kampf, The Nazi Primer*, and books about Italian unrest, the 1931 invasion of Manchuria, and Latin American turmoil (Bradley 1939). The "Have You Read?" column included citations of the works of the Stop Hitler Coalition, anti-fascist articles, and coverage of the war in Spain and China (Brownlee 1939). Erling Hunt's editorial in October 1939 was on "The War and Teaching," arguing that war and issues must be part of social studies. Hunt also mentioned the Congressional Dies Committee, forerunner of the infamous House Un-American Activities Committee (HUAC) and its investigation of American organizations with "totalitarian connections" (Hunt 1939). This activity foreshadowed an impending social crisis with direct impact on social studies teaching—the McCarthy period.

In 1939, NCSS President Ruth West sought a Board of Directors' action on a policy on "the teaching of social studies in troubled days such as these" (West 1939). The NCSS archives contain no record of that policy, but the board was often responsive to such recommendations. And the NCSS had a working committee on War and Education at that time. Announcements of the upcoming 1939 NCSS annual meeting, however, showed no concern about any social crises, but at the 1940 annual meeting, lunch sessions were added on propaganda education and Germany and the European peace.

NCSS's interest in the coming world crisis and the threats to academic freedom increased as war came closer to the United States. A joint meeting of NCSS with the American Political Science Association and the AHA in December 1939 addressed the topic "History Teachers in War Time." James Michener (1940) responded to complaints that administrators were threatening teachers with dismissal for discussing the war by stating that nothing was more important in schools than open discussion of America's part in the war. NCSS was challenged to have open discussion of the war at its Syracuse meeting in November 1940 (Anderson 1940). Bessie Pierce, known for her courageous 1930s analyses of patriotic organizations and their efforts to control and censor the social studies, advocated that teachers become more active protecting their freedom in such discussions (Pierce 1940). And NCSS approved appointment of a committee on civil rights and academic freedom. A moderate and qualified resolution was passed at the 1940 NCSS meeting stating that the "high duty of social studies teachers in the present critical world is to support all reasonable measures for national defense" (NCSS 1941).

Howard R. Anderson's presidential address of 1940 was a response to an American Legion Magazine characterization of social studies as propaganda for revolution, but Anderson felt compelled to cite his own enlistment record for World War I as credentials for his statement (Anderson 1941). Patriotic organizations had attacked social studies and supported nationalistic American history teaching for many years, but the impending war and communist scares provided these groups increased public credibility for those attacks. An NCSS committee on Academic Freedom, chaired by historian Merle Curti, reported numerous recent attacks on social studies textbooks by such groups as the American Legion and the National Association of Manufacturers (NCSS: Committee 1940).

The NCSS organizational structure included a working committee on War and Education before 1939, but little is available about their work. In September 1942, NCSS established a committee of one hundred notable social educators on Wartime Policy to prepare a statement on the role of the social studies. That policy, adopted in November 1942, was published in *Social Education* and issued as a sixteen-page pamphlet titled *The Social Studies Mobilize for Victory* (1943). It became one of the most popular publications of NCSS. This thoughtful and clear document stated that the social studies program was "essential to the war effort" and must emphasize such topics as democracy, American traditions, world issues, and human diversity. It also had an enlightened section titled "Racial and National Hatred must be Attacked."

It is apparent that NCSS was actively involved in World War II concerns, primarily in support of American governmental efforts. The U.S. War Department praised Wilbur Murra, NCSS Executive Secretary, for advising on military pre-induction training, and NCSS established a Pre-induction Training Committee to recommend citizenship education in wartime. The NCSS also was seriously concerned about threats to academic freedom and good social studies education by increasingly vocal patriotic organizations, congressional investigations, and critics of progressive education.

Following the Allied victory, NCSS approached the postwar era with a spirit of cautious optimism. *Social Education* editor Erling Hunt's October 1945 column built upon the themes in *The Social Studies Look Beyond the War*, citing the increased need to educate for a world citizenry with a decided emphasis on "waging peace," which required construction of "both the informational base and superstructure of understanding and attitudes that are essential if the needs are to be met by an informed and intelligent citizenry" (Hunt 1945, 246). Coordinated with this international emphasis was an equally significant focus on national goals, particularly the commitment to improved intercultural education, the study of democratic values and institutions, the development of economic security and individual well-being, and means by which the likelihood of war could be lessened through policy analysis.

This "vision" of post war social education blended well with the key elements of one of the most powerful vision statements of America's post war role, Henry Luce's "The American Century." Written when the outcome of World War II was unknown, but imbued with a peculiarly American sense of optimism and missionary zeal, Luce viewed the United States as ready to "create the first great American Century." To achieve this vision, Luce said, Americans had to envision the United States in four interrelated roles for the remainder of the twentieth century:

America as the dynamic center of ever-widening spheres of enterprise, America as the training center of the skillful servants of mankind, America as the Good Samaritan …and America as the powerhouse of the ideas of Freedom and Justice …" (Luce, quoted in Williams, ed., 1985)

Yet to what degree were the similar emphases of Hunt and Luce reflected in the activities and policies of NCSS, notably during periods of intense social crisis? Examination of *Social Education* from 1945 to 1970 sheds light on the extent to which NCSS advocated these emphases in its flagship publication, particularly in relation to three social crises: the anti-communist hysteria of the period 1947-1957, the civil rights movement, and the Vietnam War.

Anti-Communist Hysteria

By 1947, NCSS was identifying concerns about restrictions on the freedom to learn, as reflected in a resolution from the 1946 NCSS annual meeting. NCSS held that "learning can be free only when schools and teachers are free to teach the truth, to discuss all social and political theories and organizations, and when school programs are not burdened by the intrusion of the propaganda of pressure groups" (NCSS 1947, 5). NCSS also expressed concerns about improving the "status and respectability of the teaching profession," particularly through "recognition by boards of education and the public of the rights and privileges of teachers as individuals to exercise complete freedom in political and social conduct" (NCSS 1947, 6). As Congress and

the Executive Branch implemented measures between 1945 and 1950 designed to restrict the activities of "subversive" organizations and individuals, NCSS would return to these important themes in a series of editorials and articles to support the maintenance of academic freedom.

When anti-communist agitation became government policy, pressures at many levels of public education to restrict academic freedom became more intense, and NCSS took public exception to these trends. In an October 1948 editorial column, Lewis Paul Todd asserted,

Free men must have access to facts, for without them valid conclusions cannot be drawn and there remain only distortions and falsehood. Free men must also be permitted to draw their own conclusions. Denial of this right is denial of democracy. We must not let it happen in our classrooms (Todd 1948, 246).

Todd also advocated that educators and citizens should employ reasoned, thoughtful action to defend the principles of academic freedom, particularly in defending educators and textbooks from unwarranted attacks by "well-meaning but ill-advised citizens and civic groups." (Todd 1948) By January 1949, Todd's editorial column included a lengthy explanation of the rights and responsibilities embodied in the concept of "academic freedom," followed by a reiteration of NCSS's "determination to stand in the front lines of the continuing battle for academic freedom" (1949).

The NCSS Committee on Academic Freedom also requested that members and other educators report to it instances of limitations placed on academic freedom, how it had been protected, and what the rights and responsibilities were that educators believed were critical for the continuation of academic freedom in the schools. Taking a proactive posture, Todd suggested that local teacher organizations create their own academic freedom committees to exercise leadership in promoting academic freedom concerns, and in educating the public to reduce ignorance and misunderstanding. Five resolutions adopted by NCSS at the 1948 annual meeting addressed academic freedom issues; particularly important were those opposing loyalty oaths and loyalty probes, condemning bans on specific magazines in the schools, and supporting the right of teachers to join organizations of their choice. These concerns would loom large in major Supreme Court decisions of the period, reflecting the serious implications of government policy that restricted first amendment freedoms.

An interesting shift in tone had occurred by 1950 in the pages of *Social Education*, notably in Todd's editorial columns. The April 1950 "Editor's Page" included a substantial excerpt from the U.S. Commissioner of Education's annual report from 1949, in which the Commissioner endorsed the Educational Policies Commission's recommendation that "members of the Communist Party of the United States should not be employed as teachers." Todd stopped short of endorsing the Commissioner's position, but took no clear position himself on the issue. He raised this critical question: "how can education protect itself against those who would destroy it and at the same time safeguard the vital principle of free speech?" (Todd 1950a, 149). But Todd failed to take a forthright position about the Commissioner's opposition to the employment of communists in the schools, preferring to reprint a section of the Commissioner's report that warned against "the establishing of thought-control and the limitation of academic freedom in our schools and colleges" (Todd 1950a, 150). The apparent contradiction between restricting who was eligible to teach in the schools and advocating academic freedom did not inspire a virulent NCSS response.

The contents of Todd's editorials about communism became increasingly aligned with anti-communist sentiments, such as his support for the Truman administration's Korean War policy (Todd 1950b and 1950c) and his promotion of anti-communist teaching materials in a February 1952 column entitled "Teaching About Communism." Gone was the support for the free exchange of ideas, and in its place were statements such as: "The enemy is communism. We should know our enemy and know ourselves. This knowledge, like our military might, is an essential part of our defense program, a form of armament we dare not neglect" (Todd 1952, 51). Todd concluded his column with the admonition "Know your enemy. Know yourself. This is our surest method of defense, our safest guide along the road to larger freedom." But in the process, Todd's stance had markedly shifted to support for a "politically correct" view of academic freedom, where communists in the classroom (if not in the bedroom or the boardroom) were unacceptable, no matter the cost to freedom of inquiry.

The work of the NCSS Committee on Academic Freedom became more prominent in the pages of *Social Education*, commencing in 1950 and continuing through 1954. Beginning with a position statement on "The Treatment of Controversial Issues in the Schools" (NCSS Committee on Academic Freedom 1951), a series of articles concerning academic freedom issues authored by the committee's members were included in *Social Education*. Ruth Wood Gavian (1952) penned a strong defense of the freedom to learn in the December 1952 issue, which was followed by articles about censorship in learning materials in the February and April 1953 issues authored by T. Serviss (1953) and J. Ahrens (1953).

NCSS resolutions concerning academic freedom were regularly reported in winter issues of the journal, based upon actions taken by the organization at its annual meeting, held in the fall of the preceding year. Resolutions supporting the core principles of academic freedom were reported in the 1950, 1952, and 1954 volumes of *Social Education*, although the 1950 resolution on the freedom of inquiry contained language that could be interpreted as supporting prohibitions on communist teachers in the schools, i.e., because "it is our view that a teacher is unfit to discharge his responsibilities if, as a consequence of any attachment to other ideals, he denies himself and his students opportunity for full and free inquiry" (NCSS 1950, 32).

Also appearing in the pages of *Social Education* were Isidore Starr's analyses of recent Supreme Court decisions, ranging across a wide variety of constitutional issues. Starr reported the results of decisions about "Taft-Hartley Non-Communist Affidavit Cases," (1951a), "The State, the Teacher and Subversive Activity," (1952), and "Communism and Loyalty" (1951c). Starr presented both the majority and dissenting views of the justices before reaching his conclusions about the implications of the court's decisions for educators. This was in contrast to the narrow advocacy perspective evident in the editorials concerning communism in the schools and the employment of communists as teachers. In each article, Starr discussed the decisions within their legal and historical contexts, often employing extended excerpts from the justices' opinions to display their legal reasoning. It is noteworthy that *Social Education* included his "Recent Supreme Court Decisions" articles regularly throughout the 1950s, as they represented a comprehensive source of authoritative, well-researched analysis of academic freedom decisions for the readership.

For the remainder of the 1950s and extending into the 1960s, NCSS regularly published the resolutions of the House of Delegates (many of which took strong and unequivocal stands concerning the need to defend academic freedom) in mid-winter issues of *Social Education*. However, one searches in vain for a theme issue or coordinated set of articles during the 1950s dealing with opposing views on the issue of anti-communism in U.S. foreign policy, the impact of anti-communist domestic policies on teacher education and teacher hiring practices, or the impact of anti-communist activities in the United States on the U.S. image abroad. Numerous articles addressed cultural regions of the world, and a theme issue concerning teaching about the Soviet Union was published in April 1958. But it is abundantly clear that aside from the continuing concern for academic freedom expressed in NCSS resolutions and the regular series of Supreme Court analysis articles by Isidore Starr, NCSS failed to sustain a position on academic freedom ideals during the period 1947-1957 that would effectively uphold the Hunt/Luce vision of democratic ideals.

Civil Rights

If NCSS was inconsistent in its defense of a broadly defined view of academic freedom, its record on civil rights can only be characterized as negligent at best and indifferent at worst. During the period 1945-1949, a number of articles and news items appeared in *Social Education* about race relations, but only one editorial by William Van Til addressed such concerns (Van Til 1945). Despite the visibility of increased civil rights momentum during Truman's Fair Deal, social action by African Americans that challenged segregation and discrimination in government policies, and a series of victorious NAACP legal challenges to segregation in public facilities, there is little evidence that NCSS viewed civil rights as a central concern in its professional journal. It should be noted that two of the most distinguished African American scholars of the century, John Hope Franklin and Benjamin Quarles, did author one article each for *Social Education* between 1945 and 1950, and that both articles sought to dispel myths and stereotypes about African Americans evident in mainstream scholarship of the period (Quarles 1946; Franklin 1950). There was no emphasis on civil rights and race relations in the pages of *Social Education* comparable to that provided on teaching about the communist menace, the United Nations, or the relative merits of the core curriculum or a discipline-centered approach.

Isidore Starr once again provided the most thoughtful and penetrating work on civil rights in *Social Education* in his regular series of articles on "Recent Supreme Court Decisions." Not only did Starr address the landmark Brown vs. Board of Education of Topeka, Kansas decision in detail, he had earlier penned comprehensive pieces on racial discrimination cases in January 1951 (Starr 1951b) and January 1954 (Starr 1954a) that established the impending demise of official segregation through Supreme Court actions. Worth quoting is a section of Starr's conclusion in his article about the Brown case and related school segregation cases to illustrate his prophetic insight into the relationship of civil rights to the teaching of social education:

> The case of Brown v. Board of Education will probably take its place in our history as the most important decision in interracial relations since the Dred Scott case. In overruling a well-established and widely-accepted judicial precedent our highest tribunal asserted once more that ours is a living Constitution, flexible and sensitive to the changing conditions of a dynamic way of life. We have here another classical example of traditional legal arguments giving way before impressive data from the social sciences....(Starr 1954b, 254)

Continuing his deep concern about the importance of civil rights and race relations, Starr devoted his October 1955 article to discussing the Supreme Court's decisions about the desegregation decree designed to facilitate implementation of the Brown decision (Starr 1955).

Unfortunately, editorial pieces about civil rights and race relations seldom appeared in *Social Education* from 1950 to 1965, the period encompassing the most far-reaching policy changes in recent U.S. history concerning civil rights and the greatest achievements of the civil rights movement in dismantling discriminatory laws and practices. Only a little short of amazing was the fact that just three editorials in this entire period dealt with civil rights and race relations: one on the Brown case and its impact, the second on the relationship of the ideals of the early colonists to the conflict in values evident in the Little Rock, Arkansas, school desegration crisis, and the third addressing federal land use policy and treaty conflicts with Native Americans. In addition, there was an almost total lack of articles about civil rights in the same fifteen-year period. A theme issue on the Bill of Rights was published in December 1959, but none of the articles specifically dealt with the major aspects of the civil rights movement or the relationship of the movement to social education content and ideas.

The most compelling article of the entire period outside of the Starr court decision analyses was Supreme Court Justice William J. Brennan, Jr.'s piece on "Teaching the Bill of Rights," which made explicit reference to the dynamic nature of the constitution and its relationship to contemporary crises, such as the civil rights movement (Brennan 1963). The NCSS House of Delegates passed two resolutions on civil rights, one each in 1964 and 1965, but during these two decades there was no evidence of NCSS taking an assertive leadership role in advocating the expansion of civil rights for all Americans.

Not until 1969 did *Social Education* directly address the civil rights movement by examining the plight of African Americans and urban

Americans in two separate thematic issues (*Social Education* 1969a; *Social Education* 1969b). Some fifteen years after the Brown decision and one year after the assassination of Dr. Martin Luther King, Jr., NCSS finally took an assertive policy stand on the topic of racism and social justice, including the following statement in a Task Force Report of October 1969:

> *All deliberations and actions of the NCSS, whether they be by the House of Delegates, the Board, the officers, or the Washington staff, must be tested in respect to whether or not these actions in any way perpetuate racism and social injustice. The rationale for this position need not be stated at length since we are purely and simply referring to America's central social issue.* (NCSS 1969, 688)

Examination of any U.S. history textbook in 1994 reveals some content on the civil rights movement and the impact it had on U.S. society during the period 1945-1970. The civil rights movement that dominated domestic affairs in the United States during that quarter century commanded the attention of the world and national publics, as the nation's stated commitment to democratic ideals was tested against traditions of prejudice, ignorance, and discrimination. Hunt and Luce both recognized in the 1940s that the fulfillment of American ideals involved careful examination of core democratic values, and at its core the civil rights movement was committed to the realization of "liberty and justice for all."

NCSS, however, largely ignored the civil rights movement and in the process demonstrated indifference toward a social crisis of immense significance, one that challenged the very basis of democratic institutions and posed difficult questions for educators who daily had to confront the gap between stated ideals and social experience. Rather than leading the discussion about civil rights and seeking solutions

for problems posed by the movement, NCSS was a spectator who remained quiet as others "kept their eyes on the prize."

The Vietnam War

The Vietnam War was barely touched on in the pages of *Social Education*, and NCSS resolutions did not address the involvement of the United States in the conflict until 1969. A poem entitled "Who Am I?" was included in the theme issue on "Asia: The New, the Old, the Timeless" of November 1969, with a prefatory paragraph promising the publication of a future issue "that will present a detailed analysis of the war in Vietnam" (Vu 1969). No theme issue was published in 1970, although one article was included in May 1970: "The Dynamics of the Indochina Conflict" by Marek Thee, a reprint of an address the author had delivered at the 84th annual meeting of the American Historical Association (Thee 1970).

Although the United States was already engaged in negotiations with North Vietnam seeking a peaceful resolution to the conflict, and one could not read a newspaper, listen to the radio or watch television in the United States without hearing daily reports about the Vietnam War and its societal repercussions, there is no question that both *Social Education* and NCSS as an organization failed to respond to this monumental social crisis. Twenty-five years after Erling Hunt had called for an emphasis on "waging peace" in the pages of *Social Education*, the most serious foreign policy conflict of the post-World War II era was barely visible in the pages of the nation's leading social studies journal.

Conclusion

NCSS should be the association to which teachers look for current, insightful, and diverse views on education about contemporary and historical social crises. The necessary linkage between social crises and social studies education imposes a heavy responsibility on a professional association that aims to provide leadership to the field. That responsibility, for NCSS, includes special efforts to identify significant social crises as they develop and to: (1) communicate solid information and ideas to help educators understand the dimensions and possible consequences of the crises; (2) stimulate reasoned discourse in the field by providing a forum for widely diverse views and current and historical perspectives; (3) present thoughtful ideas for instruction; and (4) provide information and positive support on the issue of academic freedom for social studies teachers.

In examining the public actions of NCSS during the period from 1921 to 1970, we found it to have fulfilled the leadership responsibility well at certain times, as in much of its work on World War II and to some extent in the responses to McCarthy-era attacks on teachers. But there were many gaps in the work of NCSS in identifying, communicating, and providing a forum for diverse views on social crises. The Depression, civil rights, and the pre-1970 period of the Vietnam War did not receive the coverage and diversity we anticipated. And the expected, consistent, strong support for academic freedom for teachers and students to examine crises was not found, echoing the findings of Chapin and Gross in 1970 that "*Social Education* has traditionally reflected a 'kid-gloves' approach to the problems of the field" (Chapin and Gross 1970, 794). Such support is sporadic—sometimes at a high level with visible commitment, and sometimes nonexistent or hidden.

A significant goal for NCSS as it approaches the twenty-first century would be to develop systematic means for fulfilling its leadership responsibilities in relation to education about social crises. Vigorous pursuit of this goal would no doubt contribute significantly to the realization of the organization's primary stated purpose for social studies education: "to help young people develop the ability to make informed and reasoned decisions for the public good as citizens of a culturally diverse, democratic society in an interdependent world" (NCSS 1992).

Acknowledgement
The authors thank Dr. Kevin Laws of the University of Sydney, Australia, for his insightful criticism of this work.

References
Ahrens, J. "Freedom to Learn: Censorship and Learning Materials." *Social Education* 17, no. 4 (1953): 165-70.

Anderson, H. R. "The Role of Social Studies Teachers in the Present Emergency." *Social Education* 4, no. 6 (1940): 379-82.

Anderson, H. R. "The Social Studies, Patriotism, and Teaching Democracy." *Social Education* 5, no. 1 (1941): 9-14.

Barnard, J. L. "A Program for Civics Teaching for War Times and After." *The Historical Outlook* 9 (1918): 492.

Bowers, C. A. *The Progressive Educator and the Depression*. New York: Random House, 1969.

Bradley, P. "Literature of Government and Politics Abroad, 1937 and 1938." *Social Education* 3, no. 5 (1939): 327-42.

Brennan, W. J., Jr. "Teaching the Bill of Rights." *Social Education* 27, no. 5 (1963): 238-43, 256.

Brownlee, F. "Have You Read?" *Social Education* 3, no. 6 (1939): 421-25.

Chapin, J. R., and R. E. Gross. "A Barometer of the Social Studies: Three Decades of *Social Education*." *Social Education* 34, no. 7 (1970): 788-95.

Clough, N. "Making Nazis in Czechoslovakia." *Social Education* 3, no. 5 (1939): 301-306.

Crane, K. "Have You Read?" *Social Education* 3, no. 1 (1939): 77-84.

Enderis, G. "History Teaching in Nazi Germany."

The Historical Outlook 24, no. 6 (1933): 300.

Franklin, J. H. "The Teaching of American Negro History." *Social Education* 14, no. 7 (1950): 310-13, 319.

Gavian, R. W. "Freedom to Learn." *Social Education* 16, no. 8 (1952): 359-60.

Hunt, E. "Editor's Page." *Social Education* 3, no. 7 (1939): 450.

Hunt, E. "Waging Peace." *Social Education* 9, no. 6 (1945): 245-46.

Joint Commission on the Emergency in Education of the National Education Association. "The Depression and the Schools." *The Historical Outlook* 24, no. 6 (1933): 326-28.

Luce, H. "The American Century." In *America in Vietnam: A Documentary History*, edited by W. A. Williams, T. McCormick, L. Gardner, and W. LaFeber, 22-27. Garden City, N.Y.: Anchor, 1985.

Michener, J. "Discussion in Schools." *Social Education* 4, no. 1 (1940): 4, 5.

Morrissett, L. N. "The High School in the Age of Depression." *The Historical Outlook* 23, no. 6 (1932): 272-76.

National Council for the Social Studies. "NCSS Organization Chart." NCSS Archives, 1939-1940.

National Council for the Social Studies. "NCSS Resolution." *Social Education* 5, no. 1 (1941): 57.

National Council for the Social Studies. "NCSS Resolutions, 1946." *Social Education* 11, no. 1 (1947): 5-7.

National Council for the Social Studies. "Resolutions." *Social Education* 14, no. 1 (1950): 32.

National Council for the Social Studies. "Resolutions." *Social Education* 28, no. 3 (1964): 158-59.

National Council for the Social Studies. "Resolutions." *Social Education* 29, no. 3 (1965): 174-75.

National Council for the Social Studies. "Task Force Report." *Social Education* 33, no. 6 (1969): 687-96.

National Council for the Social Studies. "Definition of the Social Studies." Position Statement of the NCSS Board of Directors, 1992 .

National Council for the Social Studies: Committee. "Draft Statement on Academic Freedom." NCSS Archives, 1940.

National Council for the Social Studies: Committee on Academic Freedom. "The Treatment of Controversial Issues in the Schools." *Social Education* 15, no. 5 (1951): 232-36.

"Notes and News." *Social Education* 3, no. 1 (1939): 55-57.

Pierce, B. "The Role of Social Studies Teachers in the Present Emergency." *Social Education* 4, no. 8 (1940): 529-30.

Quarles, B. "Revisionist Negro History." *Social Education* 10, no. 3 (1946): 101-104.

Serviss, T. "Freedom to Learn: Censorship in Learning Materials." *Social Education* 17, no. 2 (1953): 65-70.

Sherwood, H. "The Relation of the United States to the Sino-Japanese Dispute." *The Historical Outlook* 24, no. 6 (1933): 180-84.

Theme issue on "Black Americans and the Social Studies." *Social Education* 33, no. 4 (1969): 385-496.

Theme issue on "Social Studies and the Urban Crisis." *Social Education* 33, no. 6 (1969): 643-760.

"The Social Studies Mobilize for Victory." *Social Education* 7, no. 1 (1943): 3-10.

Starr, I. "Recent Supreme Court Decisions: Taft-Hartley Non-Communist Affidavit Cases." *Social Education* 15, no. 2 (1951): 75-77, 81 [1951a].

Starr, I. "Recent Supreme Court Decisions: Racial Discrimination Cases." *Social Education* 15, no. 1 (1951): 13-15, 20 [1951b].

Starr, I. "Recent Supreme Court Decisions: Communism and Loyalty." *Social Education* 15, no. 7 (1951): 327-30 [1951c].

Starr, I. "Recent Supreme Court Decisions: The State, the Teacher and Subversive Activity." *Social Education* 16, no. 7 (1952): 309-11.

Starr, I. "Recent Supreme Court Decisions: Racial Discrimination." *Social Education* 18, no. 1 (1954): 10-14 [1954a].

Starr, I. "Recent Supreme Court Decisions: Public School Segregation Cases." *Social Education* 18, no. 6 (1954): 251-54 [1954b].

Starr, I. "Recent Supreme Court Decisions:

The Desegregation Decree." *Social Education* 19, no. 6 (1955): 257-58.

Thee, M. "The Dynamics of the Indochina Conflict." *Social Education* 34, no. 5 (1970): 519-24, 542.

Todd, L. P. "Who Burns Books?" *Social Education* 12, no. 6 (1948): 245-46, 258.

Todd, L. P. "Academic Freedom." *Social Education* 13, no. 1 (1949): 5-8.

Todd, L. P. "A Page from the Annual Report of the Commissioner of Education." *Social Education* 14, no. 4 (1950): 149-50 [1950a].

Todd, L. P. "Korea." *Social Education* 14, no. 7 (1950): 293 [1950b].

Todd, L. P. "Beyond Korea." *Social Education* 14, no. 8 (1950): 339-40, 354 [1950c].

Todd, L. P. "Teaching about Communism." *Social Education* 16, no. 2 (1952): 51-52.

Van Til, W. "The Task of Intercultural Education." *Social Education* 9, no. 8 (1945): 341-44.

Vu, Tru. Translated by Nguyen Ngoc Bich. "Who Am I?" *Social Education* 33, no. 7 (1969): 837.

"The War Issues Course." *The Historical Outlook* 9, no. 8 (1918): 438.

West, R. "Letter to NCSS Board of Directors." NCSS Archives (November 13, 1939).

Winter, C. "A Unit on Peace." *Social Education* 3, no. 1 (1939): 33-36.

NCSS *and Elementary School Social Studies*

John Jarolimek
University of Washington, Seattle

THE PLACE OF ELEMENTARY SCHOOL SOCIAL STUDIES IN THE NATIONAL Council for the Social Studies (NCSS) has always been just fuzzy enough to make it curiously interesting. None of the founders of the organization had a career identification with elementary education. Yet the organization, from its beginning, extended a cordial welcome to the elementary school contingent of its membership and, indeed, has actively recruited members from the ranks of elementary school teachers. Moreover, the NCSS leadership through the years seems to have been strongly influenced by the philosophy and importance of elementary school social studies. In a few cases, scholars whose academic preparation and experience were entirely at the secondary school or college level made what almost amounted to career moves to elementary education. Two of the best known were Edgar B. Wesley (originally secondary education and history) and Lawrence Senesh (university-level economics), but the reader will be able to identify many others as well. As we look at NCSS today, it is clear that social studies educators whose careers are tied to the elementary school have carved out a significant niche for themselves over the past seventy-five years.

Elementary Education and Social Studies

By whatever criteria used, one would have to conclude that NCSS is a professional organization largely focused on the needs and concerns of secondary school teachers. Indeed, most of its elected and appointed leadership has come from secondary school or college-level teaching backgrounds. That pattern is understandable because most of the members also come from that population. Yet, the concept of "social studies" as an integrated field of study is considerably more suited to the organizational format and professional orientation of the elementary school.

Although there have been persistent efforts over the last seventy-five years to encourage the development of a secondary school curriculum that would in some legitimate sense be considered an integrated field of social studies, the curriculum remains pretty much a single discipline-focused operation. The elementary school curriculum, on the other hand, has throughout this century had some characteristics of an integrated approach that is more in line with the concept of social studies as an academic field. It is precisely for this reason that many scholars have recognized the enormous potential for genuine social studies education during the elementary school years.

Leaders of NCSS, whatever their academic background, have also recognized the importance of early beginnings in civic and citizenship education. On a more or less regular basis, we find leaders reminding the membership of the importance of recruiting members from the ranks of elementary school teachers. As early as 1937, Erling M. Hunt, then editor of *Social Education*, in his report on the 1936 Detroit annual meeting wrote, "The importance and too much neglected subject of social studies in the elementary school was profitably discussed in a meeting of which Miss Mary Kelty was chairman" (Hunt 1937). Later (in 1944) Hunt reported to the membership, "More articles concerned with the elementary school … are needed" (1945). Then again in 1946 he commented on the progress and future of NCSS on the occasion of its twenty-fifth anniversary: "We have never found a way adequately to serve teachers in the elementary grades. The problem is difficult, for they are usually concerned with several other fields as well as social studies" (Hunt 1946).

The role of the elementary school teacher in a self-contained classroom is indeed very different from that of his or her secondary school counterpart. The secondary school teacher must, if only for certification requirements, be something of a specialist in the subject field in which he or she teaches. Not so for the elementary school teacher. In their book *Teaching Social Studies in Elementary Schools*, Edgar B. Wesley and Mary A. Adams indicated that the term "social studies teacher" is not really "appropriate when applied to the elementary school teacher" (1946). So much of elementary school teachers' time and effort are dedicated to teaching literacy and other basic skills that their professional interests naturally are pulled in the direction of professional organizations concerned with reading, language arts, or mathematics. It has not been easy, therefore, to recruit them in large numbers for membership in NCSS.

NCSS Reaches Out to Elementary School Teachers

NCSS, nonetheless, has been diligent in its concern for elementary school social studies and in its desire to serve the teachers of that level. For several years, it had a standing committee on elementary education whose mission was to advise the Board of Directors of the professional needs of elementary school teachers in the field of social studies. Long before NCSS required that one member of the Board of Directors be an elementary school teacher, nominating committees almost without exception included one or more candidates from the elementary school level. Ever since the mid-1930s, when NCSS began holding its annual meetings separate from the American Historical Association, the programs have included special sections dealing with the concerns of elementary school teachers. Visits to classrooms in the vicinity and "hands-on" demonstrations of teaching methodologies have been a regular part of the annual meeting programs for many years. Some kind of a status goal must certainly have been achieved with the

1961 annual meeting when the second general session consisted of five assemblies: Economics, Geography, History, Political Science, *and* Elementary Education. Section meetings devoted to elementary school social studies traditionally have been prominently featured in the programs of NCSS annual meetings.

The programs during the 1967-1972 years were particularly strong in their emphasis on elementary school social studies. It was during that period that the heavily funded curriculum development projects were at their peak. Because many dealt with elementary school social studies, the annual meeting provided an ideal forum for reporting and disseminating the findings of those projects. There can be little doubt that these programs stimulated an enormous amount of dialog among social studies professionals regarding curriculum revision and reform. They also established the intellectual groundwork for the great deal of work on scope and sequence that was to occupy the membership a decade later.

In addition to its national and regional programs, NCSS reached out to its elementary school constituency through its broad-based publications program. Until 1976, the premier publication of the organization was its yearbook, two of which were devoted exclusively to elementary school social studies. The Twelfth Yearbook, titled *The Social Studies in the Elementary School*, published in 1941, was edited by William E. Young, then Director of the Division of Elementary Education of the State Department of Education in New York. The Thirty-Second Yearbook, published in 1962, titled *Social Studies in Elementary Schools*, was edited by John U. Michaelis of the University of California, Berkeley. In addition, many of the yearbooks included one or more chapters that suggested applications of the subject matter specifically to the elementary school social studies program.

After 1976, NCSS stopped publishing yearbooks and put more of its resources into small-er, more diverse publications in the form of bulletins, "How to Do It" pamphlets, and the curriculum series. These documents could be produced more quickly than could yearbooks, which made it possible for NCSS to respond to teachers' need for current information on rapidly emerging professional issues. The documents covered a wide range of subjects and topics—from research applications to classroom methodology to substantive information on such timely topics as diversity, racism, sexism, drugs, multiculturalism, mainstreaming, and global perspectives. Taken together, these publications have provided the elementary school teacher with a collection of helpful and stimulating professional literature with immediate application to classroom practice.

The third dimension of NCSS's publication program that has spoken to the elementary school teacher are the two journals, *Social Education* and *Social Studies and the Young Learner*. As noted earlier, the editors of *Social Education* have had a history of seeking articles that treat topics of interest to elementary school teachers, and it has been a long-standing policy to have elementary school representation on the advisory board of the journal. From time to time, *Social Education* has published a special section on elementary education, thereby providing in-depth treatment of a topic. This feature became more or less institutionalized as a regular section in November 1966 when the editors inaugurated the "Elementary Education Supplement." The supplement carried five articles on a topic related to elementary school social studies and was carried in four issues each year. This feature continued in *Social Education* until the new journal, *Social Studies and the Young Learner*, was launched with the September-October 1988 issue under the editorship of Huber M. Walsh of the University of Missouri, St. Louis.

Publication of the "Elementary Education Supplement" in *Social Education* would not have been possible without outside funding; it came from the Mary G. Kelty Fund. Mary G. Kelty was one of the most prominent educators associated with elementary school social studies in the early years of NCSS. She had been an elementary school teacher and later was head of the Social Studies Department of the State Teachers College at Oshkosh, Wisconsin (now University of Wisconsin, Oshkosh). A prolific author, Kelty contributed chapters to NCSS publications and numerous articles to *Social Education*. She was highly regarded as a presenter, was a visiting professor at many universities in the United States, and was President of NCSS in 1945. Following her death in 1964, NCSS received a bequest of $204,000 from her estate, with which it established the Mary G. Kelty Trust Fund. Income from the fund was earmarked for the purpose of servicing and promoting elementary school social studies.

A great deal of credit for the attention given to elementary school social studies in NCSS programs and publications has to be given to Merrill F. Hartshorn, executive secretary from 1943 to 1974. NCSS was in its fifty-third year at the time of his retirement, and he had served as executive secretary for thirty-one of those years! Although his own professional background was not in elementary education, he had a deep appreciation for its importance. Hartshorn was also, as we would say today, "well connected": he knew personally, on a first-name basis, many of the prominent educators who were shaping the direction of elementary school social studies. In fact, he doubtless knew more persons associated with the entire field of social studies than any other individual in the country. At least partly because of Hartshorn's influence, NCSS was able to recruit top-notch intellectual resources for promoting programs and publications relating to elementary school social studies.

Even though the Council took active measures to engage elementary school teachers in its programs and publications efforts, one would have to conclude that these efforts were only partially successful. When there were NCSS national or regional meetings in their vicinity, elementary school teachers from the local area attended them in fairly large numbers. And, indeed, they were usually pleased with what they saw and heard. These teachers were conscientious about attending and participating in section meetings, and the book and equipment exhibits were seen as especially valuable to them. At NCSS conventions, it was common to see these teachers moving through the exhibit area with determination, carrying one or more bags loaded with samples, product literature, and "freebies" provided by the publishers. The impact on elementary school teachers of this exposure was, in some cases, long-standing. I know of many cases in which teachers were introduced to NCSS at one of its national or regional meetings and henceforth became faithful and regular participants. But in the majority of cases, these teachers' first brush with NCSS was also the last. When the convention left town, NCSS became little more than a memory.

Supervisors as an Important Link

One of the most effective ways in which NCSS has reached elementary school teachers has been through their supervisors. Supervisors at both the state and local levels have always played a significant role in shaping educational practice in schools.[1] Many have also been heavily involved in NCSS, and a few have served as President and Board members. The supervisors typically have a stronger than average professional drive and have earned advanced degrees. Because of their graduate work with professors who were active in NCSS, they were motivated to become involved themselves. Many have been instrumental in forming local and state councils that became affiliates of NCSS. As a consequence, they became familiar with emerging issues in social studies education and brought that knowledge to their colleagues and teachers at the local level. Through in-service programs, these supervisors were able to bring the ideas of nationally prominent social studies educators to classroom teachers at the local level. The social studies supervisors thus provided a superb conduit to classroom teachers for the dissemination of current thought and practice in the field. Usually this meant a first-hand contact with someone significantly involved in NCSS.

The names of the supervisors listed here are representative of the hundreds of others who have, through the years, been active in NCSS and who have contributed enormously to elementary school social studies: Douglas A. Phillips, Anchorage, Alaska; Jeannette B. Moon, Atlanta, Georgia; Sara M. Fowler, Boise, Idaho; Mabel Snedaker, University of Iowa Elementary School, Iowa City; Mary A. McFarland, Parkway School District, St. Louis, Missouri; Nelda Davis, Prince Georges County, Maryland; Lillian G. Witucki, Detroit, Michigan; Adelene E. Howland, Mount Vernon, New York; Ronald O. Smith, Portland, Oregon; Allen Y. King, Cleveland, Ohio; Mildred Norris, Corpus Christi, Texas; and Jerri Sutton, Richmond, Virginia.

The Intellectual History of Elementary School Social Studies

As we examine the past seventy-five years of NCSS, it is important to call attention to the impact of the Progressive Education Movement on social studies education, particularly at the elementary school level. The scholars most centrally involved with the founding of NCSS clearly embraced much of the philosophy of progressive education. The highly respected educator, Harold Rugg, one of the founding fathers of NCSS, coauthored *The Child-Centered School* (1928), a widely read book dealing with the progressive principle of child-centered, individually oriented instruction. His coauthor was Ann Shumaker, who served as editor of *Progressive Education*, the journal of the Progressive Education Association.[2] Many social studies educators of the decades between 1920 and 1950 did their graduate studies at Teachers College, Columbia University, the University of Chicago, Ohio State University, and the University of Illinois, and were profoundly influenced by progressive thought.

The belief that the purpose of social studies is to teach a particular kind of citizenship—i.e., democratic, self-involving, participatory, soundly based on critical thinking and decision making—is directly related to progressive philosophy and is reflected in numerous NCSS publications over the past seventy-five years. The idea of the comprehensive unit of study that makes social studies the "integrating center of the elementary school curriculum" has its roots in the project method of teaching developed and promoted by William Heard Kilpatrick, a leading progressive educator. The concept that schools have the right, the responsibility, and the *obligation* to be instruments of social change is pure progressive philosophy and is reflected once again in NCSS publications.

The development of skills related to problem solving, decision making, and critical thinking is, according to numerous Council statements, a high-priority goal for social studies. The model most widely cited to attain such skills is one that comes from the acknowledged father of progressive education, John Dewey, in his book *How We Think*.

Although the Progressive Education Movement has long since disappeared over the educational horizon, some of the ideas, philosophy, and educational practices that its supporters advocated remain in the methodology of mainstream elementary school social studies today. Reference here is to specific processes that have consistently been a part of NCSS programs and publications for the past several decades: (1) the need for individual and small-group instruction; (2) wide-ranging student involvement in the learning process; (3) more discussion as opposed to telling presentation modes; (4) the need for students to use a broad, diverse range of information sources; (5) the emphasis on problem solving, inquiry, and research as teaching and learning strategies; and (6) the development of social studies programs that take into account the interests and needs of learners.

Profound changes occurred in the profession's thinking about the content and methodology of elementary school social studies during the decade of 1955-1965. These appear to be years of transition from the dominant influences of the progressive era to what was called "the new social studies." This new thrust was characterized by an entirely new set of emerging academic and social concerns ranging from multiculturalism and values education to academic fundamentalism. One of the developments of consequence during this time was the increased interest in strengthening the substantive content of social studies programs across the board, with more attention to selecting subject matter from the parent disciplines.

The elementary education constituency of NCSS played an important part in these new developments. Some of the scholars who contributed significantly to elementary school social studies through NCSS during this transition period were Ruth Ellsworth, Wayne State University, Detroit, Michigan; Harold Drummond, George Peabody College for Teachers and the University of New Mexico; Ralph C. Preston, University of Pennsylvania; W. Linwood Chase, Boston University, Massachusetts; John D. McAulay, Penn State; Wilhelmina Hill, U.S. Office of Education, Washington, D.C.; Mary Willcockson, Miami University, Oxford, Ohio; John R. Lee,

Northwestern University, Illinois; John U. Michaelis, University of California, Berkeley; Robert V. Duffey, University of Maryland; Vincent R. Rogers, University of Massachusetts; and Paul R. Hanna, Stanford University, California. Hanna is thought to be the person most closely associated with the "expanding horizons" curriculum sequence for elementary school social studies.

Following 1965, there was a firestorm of activity directed toward the revision and reconstruction of the social studies curriculum. Much of this work was focused on the elementary school. Some of the scholars named in the previous paragraph were also an important part of this movement, and many were associated with various curriculum research and development projects underway at the time. One of the prominent educators of the post-1965 period frequently cited in educational literature was Hilda Taba who, along with her colleagues and students at San Francisco State and in Contra Costa County, California, did extensive work on concept development in social studies. Taba had long been associated with NCSS and served on the Board of Directors in the early 1940s. She was a popular presenter at NCSS meetings and was very influential in shaping the direction of social studies in the late 1960s and 1970s.

During the 1970s and 1980s, many new names and faces began appearing with increasing frequency on NCSS programs and in the NCSS professional literature. A few of them are Theodore Kaltsounis, James A. Banks, and Walter C. Parker, University of Washington, Seattle; William W. Joyce and Janet Alleman, Michigan State University, East Lansing; Edith King, University of Denver; Mark C. Schug, University of Wisconsin, Milwaukee; Peter H. Martorella, North Carolina State University, Raleigh; Dorothy J. Skeel, George Peabody-Vanderbilt University, Nashville; Virginia A. Atwood, University of Kentucky, Lexington; Charlotte

Crabtree, University of California, Los Angeles; Bruce R. Joyce, Columbia University, New York; Val E. Arnsdorf, University of Delaware, Newark; Murry R. Nelson, Penn State, University Park; Huber M. Walsh, University of Missouri, St. Louis; Jesus Garcia, University of Illinois, Champaign; John T. Mallan, Syracuse University, New York; Richard A. Diem, University of Texas at San Antonio; Everett T. Keach, Jr., University of Georgia, Athens; O. L. Davis, Jr., The University of Texas at Austin; David A. Welton, Texas Tech University, Lubbock; and Wayne L. Herman, Jr., University of Maryland, College Park. Several of these professionals are currently at the peak of their careers in social studies education, and will no doubt remain active through the 1990s and into the 2000s. In a number of cases they also have graduate students who are following in their footsteps and are prepared to keep elementary school social studies on the cutting edge of concern in NCSS well into the next century.

Looking to the Future

This new generation of leaders will be facing some extraordinarily complex challenges in the years ahead. As long as elementary school social studies retained as its defining attributes those that evolved from its roots during the progressive era, teachers, supervisors, curriculum developers, textbook authors, and other professionals, including NCSS leaders, were comfortable in believing that they knew what the dimensions, mission, and basic structure of this field were. With the developments of the past three decades, however, much of the earlier consensus concerning the basic nature of elementary school social studies has been fractured.

The present situation is also complicated by the strong promotion of narrow and sometimes unenlightened self-interest, coupled with an absolute unwillingness to accept compromise. Many issues have become politicized to the extent that curriculum decisions may not always be made on their educational merit but on the amount of power a group can marshal to influence decision makers. Thus, leadership from NCSS is more often than not eclipsed by that of other concerned groups. Social studies programs are today being shaped by competing constituencies who want to see the curriculum developed around what they believe to be important—whether that is one of the social science disciplines, i.e., history, geography, economics, civics; or social causes such as multiculturalism, diversity, ethnicity, gender; or other issues associated with the "political correctness" phenomenon. NCSS today is experiencing some loss of status and credibility in this competitive arena partly as a result of the reluctance of its intellectual leadership two decades ago to close ranks and present a united front on the meaning, mission, and structure of elementary school social studies.

Most social studies professionals would doubtless agree that the programs of the past are not adequate for the incredibly complex, fast-moving, globally oriented life in which we live today. On the other hand, we have not, either as a profession or as a society, moved anywhere close to consensus on the shape and structure of social studies programs that *are* adequate. Thus, the challenge facing this and the next few generations of social studies leaders will be to fashion programs that incorporate those essential elements that are critical to democratic citizenship in a post-modern world.

A Personal Conclusion

If the reader will indulge me, I should like to conclude this essay with a few personal comments. My own life exactly covers the life span of the National Council for the Social Studies. Because NCSS and I were both born in 1921, we have, in a sense, grown up together. I have known personally fifty-one of the organization's presidents and all of its executive secretaries. I served as President myself in 1971, the year of the Council's Golden Anniversary. I first became active as a program participant in 1959 at the meeting held at the Muehlebach Hotel in Kansas City at which the former President Harry S. Truman was the banquet speaker.

I remember that meeting well because W. Linwood Chase, whom I did not know prior to that time, took me under his wing, introduced me to many individuals at the meeting, and provided me with an enormously helpful—and enthusiastic—orientation to the organization. He was a past President, seemed to know everyone, and was regarded as a genuine heavyweight in the organization. His concern for me was a professional courtesy that only a true gentleman would be willing to extend. His kindness kindled a warmth in my heart for the National Council for the Social Studies that continues to this day.

Notes

1 The term "supervisor" is used here in the broad sense to include consultants, assistant superintendents, curriculum directors, and other designations for individuals in positions of responsibility for the direction and supervision of instruction.

2 Rugg later authored a series of social studies textbooks for the elementary school grades that were based on the concept of "fusion" or integration of subject matter. Additionally, the subject matter for the books was selected on the basis of what citizens presumably needed to know. The series, initially published at Rugg's own expense, became an immediate success and was soon taken over by Ginn and Co. By 1940, the books were in deep trouble because the philosophy on which they were based conflicted with the prevailing social attitudes and political climate. The project crashed as quickly as it had skyrocketed.

References

Hunt, E. M. "Notes and News." *Social Education* 1 (1937): 54.

_____. "Notes and News." *Social Education* 9 (1945): 38.

_____. "Editor's Page." *Social Education* 10 (1946): 8.

Rugg, H., and A. Shumaker. *The Child-Centered School.* New York: World Book, 1928.

Wesley, E. B., and M. A. Adams. *Teaching Social Studies in Elementary Schools.* Boston: D.C. Heath, 1946.

NCSS
The Years Ahead

O. L. Davis, Jr.
The University of Texas at Austin

ONLY FIVE YEARS REMAIN IN THIS CENTURY. AT THE END OF THAT time, not only will the century change; a new millennium will ensue. One thousand-year period will end, and a fresh thousand years will begin. Such calendar changes, especially millennial anticipations, carry with them the prospects for awesome, even radical change, and certainly opportunities for altered lives and visions.

Within this context, proper observance of the seventy-fifth anniversary of the National Council for the Social Studies (NCSS) may responsibly include self-conscious attention to its long-term future. The ordinary assumptions of continuance are possibly insufficient. So, also, routine questions about the Council's years ahead may be inadequate. To consider possibilities for only its next five years or even the twenty-five years in advance of the NCSS centenary may not allow it to harvest all its possible fruits in the years ahead. On the other hand, maybe only short-term planning represents a reasonable possibility. Our imagination may be inadequate to consider the scope of a century, much less a millennium. Indeed, even to consider such long-term concerns can divert attention from real next steps and paralyze mindful consideration of practical opportunity. The reality of the conclusion of this century and millennium, nevertheless, will not disappear. Their recognition must intensify consideration of the future. The times make a difference.

How will NCSS recognize and imagine the practice of social studies teachers in the years ahead? How will it understand the realities of changed social studies offerings in the emerging American school curriculum? How will it come to know the professional concerns of social studies teachers, and how will it assist those teachers in their perception of fresh opportunities? How will it improve its service to members and to the larger interests of the social studies? Responses to these and other questions that issue from them will clearly shape the nature of NCSS in the years ahead. Some of these considerations will revisit previous deliberations; others likely will be new.

Toward the Discovery of the Future

For the tasks ahead, no chart or map is available. This presumed difficulty, however, is only a commonplace of ordinary life. Even without a chart, both directions and landmarks are known; they can be recognized and considered. And without a map, opportunities for discovery emerge.

Three categories of concern suggest the deliberations that NCSS should encourage in the near term.

Stability and Growth

Voluntary associations like NCSS seem routinely plagued with more suggestions for new programs than they have funds with which to translate ideas into reality. Most also enjoy only a small corps of loyal, continuing members. Many current NCSS members are not expected to routinely renew their memberships over a long period of years. Without a stable and, in fact, a steadily increasing membership, NCSS and other voluntary groups can seldom broaden their outreach as they wish. Sometimes, they exist only precariously. Few NCSS members, now and in the past, are aware of the organization's severely restrictive budgetary constraints. Members take for granted that their journal and other services will arrive on a timely basis.

However, a non-profit organization is governed by the same economic rules applicable to for-profit businesses. For NCSS to continue its work, its income at least must match its expenses. To account for costs over which NCSS has no control, income must increase almost every year. To embark on new ventures, additional revenue will be required. For NCSS to increase its membership, especially its continuing membership, and thereby its income, is a necessity.

Members, therefore, should expect various initiatives to increase the organization's income. For periods of time, decisions to curtail some usual programs may enable funds to be directed to other activities that will generate increased revenue. Membership growth and financial stability constitute sure prerequisites to continuance as well as to expansion and development of programs.

For many years, NCSS leaders have recognized that current members represent only a small fraction of the nation's social studies teachers. NCSS has attempted a variety of recruitment procedures, some of which have enjoyed more success than others. Efforts must continue to attract increasing numbers of social studies teachers to membership and expanded participation. NCSS certainly must not settle easily for a small enrollment.

Another aspect of growth relates to the need for increased diversity among the NCSS membership and leadership. Crucially, the changing ethnic composition of American teachers must continue to be reflected in decisions about leadership, from committee chairs to president. Committees and awards related to multiculturalism were important early steps for the Council. Additional actions now are necessary for NCSS to translate its own official expressions of high purpose to certain reality.

The Nature of the Social Studies and NCSS

A number of NCSS members, including individuals on various governance bodies, have invested much time during recent years to the development of a "definition" of the field. Adoption of this definition as official policy, however, seems unlikely to forestall subsequent discussion and, in time, revision. The fact is that, in the reality of school practice, the issue remains unsettled and the official statement seems less than helpful.

Regardless of official definition, social studies in most American schools remains a term that describes a cluster of course offerings—not a particular course or set of courses. Even when the term is listed as a course, pupils and adults (teachers, parents, school board members) typically understand it as an offering that stresses mainly history and geography. Not only partisan advocates of a unitary social studies, but also its increasingly public and hostile detractors, ordinarily misunderstand or misrepresent this fundamental commonplace of school practice.

The contemporary standards movement offers no solace to the official NCSS position. The local and national prominence of the proposed standards in history—particularly because they are so vigorously contested—focus attention on school history offerings at the expense of consideration of more inclusive purposes and understandings in the social studies standards. To be sure, debates and revisions should continue on all the current standards related to the social studies (e.g., social studies, history, geography, citizenship). The boundaries between the several social studies appear much more clearly delineated now than during most of the past seventy-five years. Deflection or cessation of deliberation about challenging standards in the field would be particularly injurious to the field and to NCSS.

Historically and practically, NCSS has served to help improve the teaching of history and the other social studies, initially in secondary schools, and more recently in elementary schools. Only in the past few years has it drawn definitions as lines in the sand. Unfortunately, these actions may well serve to exclude and/or to alienate current and potential members, such as teachers who currently teach history and want to be known as history teachers. In addition, the current definition marginalizes citizenship as a function only of the social studies rather than emphasizing it as the central purpose of public schooling in this democracy. The costs to NCSS of the current political definition seem inordinately high in exchange for only professed benefits.

Of course, school social studies and NCSS must contribute properly to a powerfully enriched civic education for young Americans. These contributions to civic education, however, are not restricted to "civics education" or "citizenship education." Certainly, they must include attention to special emphases and tasks, problems and issues, and even some courses. They also should include more lively and substantive offerings in the several social studies. Although the social studies and NCSS should be prominent, even major, contributors to the civic educational purposes of public schools, neither may claim to encompass the entirety, or even the heart, of the schools' general concern for civic education. A re-envisioned social studies is necessary.

Continuing reconsideration of the practical nature of social studies in American schools can enable NCSS to reestablish itself as an appropriate and welcoming home to teachers of social studies. In the absence of any particular educational orthodoxy, NCSS can reassert its provision of a common meeting ground for all social studies teachers.

Advocacies, Emphases, and NCSS

The context of social studies in American schools has always been influenced by contemporary social events as well as by recent scholarship in the several disciplines that underlie social studies. This condition surely will continue. Within this context, both the social studies curriculum and NCSS can profit—but not without mindful attention to priorities. Four concerns illustrate this point.

Patriotism

Throughout the history of NCSS, advocates in the general public as well as in the ranks of teaching have called for patriotism to be central or at least explicit in the role of both schools and social studies. Wartime needs for national unity and the excesses of the Cold War formed the basis for this advocacy, which was frequently harsh and strident in nature. In the intervals between national crises, concern about patriotism languished on the margins of programs and concerns. Many individuals—teachers and non-teachers—denigrated patriotism as a sentiment unworthy of Americans, especially for pupils in schools. The up-and-down history of explicit attention to patriotism in the social studies curriculum and by NCSS marks its transient prominence. This record also illustrates its convenience as a brutal bludgeon in debates and public attacks about the purposes and adequacy of social studies programs. During different "red scares" in a number of local situations, from Pasadena to Seattle to Houston to New York, a number of teachers suffered grievously, and programs were savaged. Surely, NCSS can improve its service to members in the years ahead by encouraging sustained and thoughtful attention to issues of patriotism in American democracy and in the social studies. That attention, to be fruitful, must avoid both simplistic jingoism and cynicism. It should also be informed by the reality that much of the political justification and public support for the inclusion of social studies in the curriculum relates to particularized national and civic purposes.

Teaching of History

NCSS has always fostered the improved teaching of history in schools, and, indeed, enjoyed a lengthy association with the American Historical Association. Nevertheless, over a number of years, some prominent NCSS members came to believe that history courses unfortunately dominated schools' social studies programs and called for profoundly changed emphases in those offerings. Most commonly proposed was the study of modern social problems, often in lieu of courses in history and other social studies (e.g., geography, economics). Advocacy for studies based on societal problems became legitimated by the overarching concern for improved citizenship education. Within the clamor for changed curriculum emphases, at least two conditions can be noted. First, schools continued to offer history courses. Secondly, the emphasis on social problems, from propaganda analysis to law-related education, waxed and waned, but found curriculum security mainly as elements of established history courses. Any suggestion that history will disappear from schools' social studies offerings seems fanciful in the extreme.

Thus, it seems only reasonable to call NCSS to pay explicit and conspicuous attention to the improvement of the teaching of history in the years ahead. Persistent problems in history teaching merit continued programmatic attention. For example, the use of sources in the teaching of history seems not to be an ideological issue of "inquiry teaching." Rather, the main practical problem for teachers in the use of sources involves the availability of appropriate sources related to specific historical events and situations. Additional problems include the often subtle meanings of the source's context, the importance of good writing to historical portrayal, the development of historical reasoning, and the nature of historical fact, narrative, conclusion, and accuracy. Particularly important, as well, is the revisionist concern for teaching history to young children. Surely, in the years ahead, NCSS should lead the way to lively history being a curriculum commonplace in American schools.

Global Education

For students to fail to engage in serious study of other peoples and nations, their problems, and the relationships of those problems to the life of Americans seems unthinkable at the present time. News of events in distant countries immediately raises questions about the impact of those events on Americans. Numerous examples indicate the variety and complexity of global concerns and the necessity that they be studied: the decline of coffee prices in Brazil, the brutal civil war in the Balkans, the civil and economic unrest in the former Soviet Union, the spread of the AIDS virus across the world from its origins in a remote village in a distant continent, the engagement of German troops as "peacekeepers" on foreign soil, and proposed changes in U.S. immigration policy. American schools and their social studies programs should offer more—not less—opportunity for deeper study of global concerns.

NCSS has substantial experience in fostering global education. Its support of the Glens Falls, N.Y., program, forty-five years ago unfortunately seems to have been forgotten. However, its recent work to expand and improve teaching about Japan has yielded an abundant harvest of individual good will and solid lessons in schools. Nevertheless, NCSS can fashion for itself a greatly expanded role in global education. In this regard, of course, more and better attention to geography, history, economics, and politics is essential, not simply desirable. That curriculum concern for global education and similar emphases not be trivialized into a minor current events segment of daily class sessions should be an assumption of serious teaching practice. Still, more is needed. Some matters in the world matter too much not to be treated by themselves on occasion. Perhaps teams of teachers using differentiated daily schedules for varying periods of time during the year are a more appropriate arrangement for such studies than are conventional methods. NCSS can serve its members by fostering continuing serious consideration of means by which pupils may study about the global village and its problems as well as about other similar concerns that cannot be squeezed into traditional courses. The issue cannot be the substitution of global education (or community service programs or multicultural emphases or the study of religion or any of a number of other important matters) for serious study of history and other social studies. Rather, NCSS can help invent means by which global education and its related band of concerns partake of some of the curriculum resources available (e.g., time, funds, space), not as afterthought but as a considered plan.

Research

For most of its history, NCSS has not emphasized mindful research relating to the curriculum and teaching of the social studies. This failure seems important for at least two reasons.

First, NCSS was formed at a time coincident with the birth of serious interest in educational research in the United States. Some of its founders, specifically Harold and Earle Rugg, conducted, sponsored, and published some of the first major research and reviews of research about the social studies. NCSS, however, conspicuously did not participate as a sponsor or supporter of this kind of research. On the other hand, throughout its seventy-five years of existence, NCSS has routinely supported the widespread dissemination of recent academic research findings, particularly in history, which teachers might use in their teaching.

Second, during the past three decades especially, NCSS has become more active in fostering research related to social studies curriculum and teaching, and students' learning of social studies. Using its recent experience as a base, NCSS can add to its encouragement and advancement of research in social studies education. This research concern is not an issue that separates school and university members, and it does not unduly focus NCSS attention on university members' self-serving concerns. Rather, it lies at the heart of the sure need to increase the knowledge available to improve the common lot of social studies in American schools.

Using a variety of legitimate research methodologies enables scholars and teachers to inquire into an increasing array of important questions. Two additional emphases seem noteworthy for the years ahead. First, the importance and popularity of school-based research, some of it collaboratively implemented and some of it led or conducted by teachers, already yields important advances in understanding serious questions. Several research matters important to the practice of teaching, some too long ignored, illustrate this concern. For example, how do students at different levels of schooling learn historical stories or accounts; historical reasoning, facts, processes, writing, and empathy; and the appropriateness and use of different types of historical sources and evidence? How do teachers work together to understand and use the recently proposed standards in the social studies? To modify and test alternative standards? To fashion increasingly robust, challenging, and exciting social studies programs? How do students at different levels of schooling engage in social action projects and learn to discuss important issues? Research attention to these kinds of questions will help social studies teachers move forward into the future. Second, the history of the social studies has become recognized as valuable and respectable only in recent years. As a consequence, some conventional wisdom already has been challenged and the promise of an informed history of our field seems altogether possible. The history of the social studies needs much vigorous research and more individuals to investigate it. The social studies has a usable past and NCSS can assist in its recovery.

These are my four areas of concern. They identify a few of the matters that properly should be early entries on a list of priority matters for NCSS as it invents its future. They also illustrate both the complexity and the opportunities for NCSS as it steps into the years ahead. As the homely expression notes, "So much to do and such little time." Beginnings, however, can be undertaken. They will make a difference. They always have.

Ready or Not: Next Steps to the Years Ahead

Perhaps the easiest response at the entrance to a new century and a new millennium is for individuals and groups to remain awesomely still: to contemplate risks, to relish past accomplishments, and to hesitate even to take one next step. That prospect, however, is empty and possible only in imagination. The National Council for the Social Studies cannot tarry on the verge of a truly uncertain future for next year, the new century, or the next thousand years. However uncertain it and its members may be, they can trust their next steps.

No map of the future is available. But a direction is clear: the pursuit of a rich, challenging, and robust social studies that will serve new generations of Americans in this democracy. With such a noble charter available, any map would be inadequate, and would probably trivialize the enterprise. On NCSS's journey into the years ahead, it surely will err from time to time. Still, if the past continues to serve as a reasonable guide, NCSS will correct its mistakes. It may take the wrong turn or lose its way for a time. During some dark nights, however, its members will take fresh star sights, reorient its journey to its true direction, and strike off once more.

Throughout its seventy-five years, NCSS has continued to move. It is stepping into its future, now.

NCSS *Contributors*

James L. Barth is Professor of Social Studies Education in the Department of Curriculum and Instruction of the School of Education at Purdue University. He is the author of numerous publications on social studies education, including many on the origins of the social studies. Dr. Barth is also Department Editor of the Foundations section of *Social Education.*

Edward Buendia is a doctoral student in the Department of Curriculum and Instruction at the University of Illinois in Champaign. Formerly an elementary school teacher, he plans to work in the field of social studies education in public schools.

O.L. Davis, Jr., is Professor of Curriculum and Instruction at the University of Texas at Austin. Previously, he was on the faculties of the University of North Carolina, Chapel Hill, and Kent State University. He has been an elementary and secondary school teacher and an elementary school principal, and has served in leadership positions in many educational associations. He is the author or co-author of over two hundred publications dealing with social studies. He is also editor of the *Journal of Curriculum and Supervision.*

William R. Fernekes is supervisor of social studies at Hunterdon Central Regional High School in Flemington, New Jersey. His many publications emphasize issues-centered education and human rights and Holocaust/ genocide education. Dr. Fernekes was also a member of the Task Force that developed *Expectations of Excellence: Curriculum Standards for Social Studies.*

Jack R. Fraenkel is Director of the Research and Development Center and Professor of Interdisciplinary Studies in the College of Education at San Francisco State University. He is the editor of *Theory and Research in Social Education.* His publications include the book *How to Design and Evaluate Research in Education*, now in its third edition, and many other books and articles on social education.

Jesus Garcia is Professor of Education in the Department of Curriculum and Instruction at the University of Illinois in Champaign, where he teaches graduate and undergraduate courses in social studies and multicultural education. The many publications which he has authored or co-authored include a U.S. history textbook for middle schools, *America's Past and Promise*, and a book and numerous articles dealing with issues of diversity.

John Jarolimek is Professor Emeritus at the University of Washington, Seattle. He has contributed extensively to NCSS publications and programs, and served as NCSS President in 1971, the year of the Council's fiftieth anniversary. Dr. Jarolimek was the first editor of the Elementary Education Supplement of *Social Education.*

Linda S. Levstik is Professor of Humanities Education at the University of Kentucky, Lexington, KY. Her scholarship and publications have focused on the development of historical thinking in elementary and middle school age children. Dr. Levstik recently co-authored the book *How Did We Get Here?*

Teaching History in Elementary and Middle Schools. She is Chairperson of the NCSS Focus Group on History Standards.

Margit E. McGuire is Professor and Chair of Teacher Education at Seattle University. She was President of the National Council for the Social Studies in 1991-92. Dr. McGuire is the author of the social studies program *Storypath*, published by Everyday Learning. In 1991, she was the recipient of Washington state's prestigious Excellence in Education Award.

Jack L. Nelson is Professor of Education at Rutgers University. The founding Chair of the College and University Faculty Assembly of NCSS, he has served as Editor of *Theory and Research in Social Education* and book review editor of *Social Education.* He has published 16 books and over 150 articles and reviews.

James P. Shaver is Dean of the School of Graduate Studies and Professor of Secondary Education at Utah State University. He was President of the National Council for the Social Studies in 1976. Dr. Shaver is the author of books and articles on a variety of educational issues. He also edited *The Handbook of Research on Social Studies Teaching and Learning*, published in 1991

Stephen J. Thornton is Associate Professor of Social Studies and Education and Chair of the Department of Languages, Literature and Social Studies in Education at Teachers College, Columbia University. He has served as Chair of the College and University Faculty Assembly of NCSS. Among the interests reflected in his recent publications is the reconsideration of patterns of curriculum and instruction.

Jan L. Tucker is Professor of Social Studies Education at Florida International University, Miami, where he is Director of the Global Awareness Program in the College of Education. He has written widely on global education issues. Dr. Tucker served as President of the National Council for the Social Studies from 1987 to 1988.